Mainframes in the Hybrid Cloud Era

Mainframes

Isaac Nangan

Published by Isaac Nangan, 2024.

MAINFRAMES IN THE HYBRID CLOUD ERA

First edition. February 10, 2024.

ISBN: 978-9815194463

Written by Isaac Nangan.

Table of Contents

To Coleen, Sky and Neo. You are my inspirations.

Mainframes in the Hybrid Cloud Era

Isaac Nangan

Preface

In the rapidly evolving world of information technology, the integration of established systems like mainframes with emerging paradigms such as the hybrid cloud represents a significant and challenging frontier. This book, "Mainframes in the Hybrid Cloud Era," is crafted to bridge the knowledge gap between these seemingly disparate worlds, providing a comprehensive guide to understanding, implementing, and optimizing mainframe systems within the hybrid cloud infrastructure.

Mainframes have long been the backbone of critical business operations for many large organizations, known for their reliability, scalability, and security. However, as cloud computing has risen to prominence, bringing flexibility, cost-efficiency, and innovative capabilities, a crucial question has emerged: How can the robustness of mainframes be harmoniously combined with the agility of cloud environments? This book aims to answer this question, presenting a balanced view that respects the legacy of mainframes while embracing the future of cloud technologies.

Throughout the chapters, we explore various facets of this integration. From the architectural considerations of combining mainframes with cloud infrastructures to the specific challenges of data management, security, and application development in a hybrid environment, the book covers a broad spectrum of topics. Each chapter is designed to provide practical insights and actionable strategies, drawn from real-world experiences and current best practices.

Moreover, this book does not merely focus on the technical aspects. It also delves into the strategic and managerial perspectives, crucial for leaders and decision-makers who need to navigate the complexities of integrating mainframe systems with cloud solutions. By providing a range of case studies and future-looking predictions, the book offers a comprehensive view of the field, beneficial for both technical professionals and business leaders.

As the author, my intention is to provide a resource that is not only informative but also accessible to a wide range of readers. Whether you are a seasoned IT professional, a student of information technology, or a business leader seeking to understand the implications of mainframe and cloud integrations, this book is for you. It is my hope that "Mainframes in the Hybrid Cloud Era" will serve as a valuable guide and reference as you navigate the exciting and challenging world of mainframe and hybrid cloud computing.

Welcome to the journey of exploring the synergistic potential of mainframes and hybrid clouds.

Prologue

At the dawn of the computer age, mainframes were the titans of computing, powering the critical operations of governments, banks, and large corporations. They were marvels of their time, symbolizing the pinnacle of technological advancement. As decades passed, the landscape of computing underwent profound transformations, with the emergence of personal computers, the internet, and eventually, cloud computing. These shifts seemed to herald the obsolescence of the mainframe, yet, paradoxically, mainframes have not only endured but also continued to play a vital role in the digital infrastructures of many organizations.

In recent years, the advent of cloud computing has revolutionized the way organizations think about data processing, storage, and access. The cloud promised unparalleled flexibility, scalability, and cost savings, enticing businesses to migrate their operations. However, this migration presented unique challenges, particularly for those deeply entrenched in mainframe technologies. The question arose: How could these seemingly antiquated yet powerful mainframes coexist with the dynamic and evolving cloud environments?

This is where the concept of the hybrid cloud comes into play, offering a bridge between the old and the new, the reliable and the innovative. The hybrid cloud model allows organizations to leverage the strengths of both mainframes and cloud systems, creating a powerful, integrated infrastructure. This fusion has opened a world of possibilities, allowing for more efficient operations, enhanced scalability, and the agility to adapt to changing business needs.

The prologue of this book sets the stage for a journey through the realms of mainframe and hybrid cloud integration. It is a story that weaves together the past, present, and future of computing, exploring how legacy systems and cutting-edge technologies can not only coexist but thrive together. As you turn the pages, you will discover the intricacies of mainframes, the versatility of cloud computing, and the myriad ways in which they can be integrated to create robust, efficient, and future-proof digital ecosystems.

This book is not just a technical guide; it is a narrative about resilience, adaptation, and the enduring relevance of mainframe technology in an age dominated by cloud computing. It's a testament to the ingenuity of engineers and IT professionals who have found innovative ways to marry tradition with transformation, ensuring that the legacy of mainframes continues to play a crucial role in the digital age.

Welcome to the prologue of "Mainframes in the Hybrid Cloud Era." Let us embark on this enlightening journey together.

Chapter 1: Introduction to Mainframes and Hybrid Cloud

Historical Overview of Mainframes

Mainframes have a storied history, dating back to the 1950s. Initially, they were massive, room-filling machines that were the heart of business computing. Early mainframes like the IBM 700/7000 series were used primarily by large institutions for critical tasks such as census calculations, banking transactions, and airline reservations. Over the years, mainframes evolved significantly in terms of size, power, and functionality. By the 1980s and 1990s, they had become smaller and more powerful, capable of handling multiple tasks simultaneously, making them indispensable for large corporations and government agencies. Despite predictions of their demise with the advent of personal computers and servers, mainframes have remained relevant due to their unparalleled reliability, security, and processing power, especially for transaction-heavy applications.

Evolution of Cloud Computing

Cloud computing, in contrast, is a more recent phenomenon, gaining significant momentum in the 21st century. It emerged from the advancements in virtualization, broadband internet, and ubiquitous access to high-capacity networks and low-cost computers. The idea was to enable users and enterprises to access computing resources as a utility, much like electricity, rather than having to own and maintain physical infrastructure. Companies like Amazon, Google, and Microsoft led the way in offering cloud services, transforming the landscape of IT infrastructure. Cloud computing is characterized by its scalability, flexibility, and the pay-as-you-go pricing model, which has made it a popular choice for businesses of all sizes. From simple data storage solutions to complex enterprise applications, cloud services have become integral to modern computing needs.

Defining Hybrid Cloud: Integration of Mainframes and Cloud Services

The hybrid cloud is a computing environment that combines the use of on-premises data centers, private clouds, and public clouds, allowing data and applications to be shared between them. When it comes to integrating mainframes into this environment, the hybrid cloud provides a bridge between the traditional mainframe architecture and the modern cloud infrastructure. This integration leverages the strength of mainframes - high-speed processing and security - with the flexibility and scalability of cloud services.

In a hybrid cloud model, mainframes often continue to handle core, mission-critical applications while interfacing with cloud-based applications and services. This setup allows organizations to modernize their IT infrastructure without completely overhauling their existing mainframe systems. The integration facilitates seamless data exchange, workload balancing, and expanded functionality, combining the best of both worlds.

For instance, an enterprise might use its mainframe for high-volume transaction processing, like financial transactions, while relying on cloud services for customer relationship management and analytics. This approach not only preserves the significant investments made in mainframe technology but also enables organizations to leverage the agility and innovation offered by cloud computing.

In summary, the integration of mainframes and cloud services within a hybrid cloud model represents a strategic approach to IT infrastructure, combining the reliability and power of mainframes with the flexibility and scalability of the cloud. This chapter sets the stage for a deeper exploration of how this integration is achieved and the benefits it brings to modern computing.

1.1. Historical Overview of Mainframes

The historical journey of mainframes is a fascinating tale of technological evolution and enduring relevance. Beginning in the 1950s, mainframes emerged as the giants of computing, dominating the business and government sectors. These early machines, like the IBM 700/7000 series, were literal behemoths, often occupying entire rooms. Their primary roles were in large-scale computations and data processing tasks, which were essential in sectors like government for census data, finance for banking transactions, and in airlines for reservation systems. This era marked the inception of mainframes as critical tools for handling vast amounts of data efficiently and securely.

As technology progressed, the 1960s and 1970s saw significant advancements in mainframe technology. IBM introduced the System/360, a revolutionary line of mainframes that offered compatibility across its models, a feature unheard of at the time. This era also witnessed the introduction of more sophisticated operating systems and the ability to support multiple programming languages, which broadened the utility of mainframes across various industries.

Entering the 1980s and 1990s, the landscape of computing began to shift dramatically with the advent of personal computers and networked servers. This period could have signaled the end of the mainframe era. However, contrary to many predictions, mainframes did not fade into obsolescence. Instead, they evolved. They became smaller, more powerful, and more energy-efficient. This era saw the transformation of mainframes into multi-functional machines capable of handling diverse tasks simultaneously – from transaction processing to complex data analytics.

One of the key reasons for the enduring relevance of mainframes is their reliability. For large corporations and government agencies, the mainframe's ability to process high volumes of transactions reliably and securely is unmatched. This is particularly crucial in sectors like banking, where transaction integrity and security are paramount.

Moreover, mainframes have continuously adapted to new technological trends. They have embraced changes such as the introduction of graphical user interfaces, the integration with distributed networks and systems, and the ability to run modern programming languages and applications. This adaptability has ensured that mainframes remain a cornerstone in the IT infrastructure of many large organizations.

In summary, the history of mainframes is not just a story of survival but one of adaptation and resilience. From room-sized machines to the compact, power-packed systems of today, mainframes have continually evolved to meet the changing needs of the digital world. Their journey reflects a constant balancing act between leveraging tried-and-tested technology and embracing innovation, ensuring that mainframes remain an integral part of the business and government IT ecosystem.

1.2. Evolution of Cloud Computing

The evolution of cloud computing represents a paradigm shift in the world of information technology. It's a journey from the constraints of physical infrastructure to the flexibility of virtualized resources, fundamentally changing how businesses and individuals access and use computing power.

The Emergence of Cloud Computing

The concept of cloud computing started to take shape in the late 1990s and early 2000s, with the advent of significant technological advancements. Key among these were:

1. **Virtualization**: This technology, which allows multiple virtual machines to run on a single physical hardware host, is the cornerstone of cloud computing. It maximized hardware utilization and provided the foundation for flexible and scalable computing resources.
2. **Broadband Internet**: The widespread availability and increased speed of broadband internet made it feasible to access data and applications hosted remotely, rather than on local servers or personal computers.
3. **High-Capacity Networks and Low-Cost Computing**: These developments made it economically viable to host and process large amounts of data off-site, in centralized locations.

Pioneers and Adoption

Early pioneers like Amazon, Google, and Microsoft recognized the potential of cloud computing and started offering services that allowed businesses and individuals to rent computing power and storage, rather than investing in expensive hardware. Amazon Web Services (AWS), launched in 2006, was a game-changer, providing a comprehensive suite of cloud services that included storage, computation, and even fully managed databases.

Characteristics of Cloud Computing

Cloud computing is characterized by several key features:

1. **Scalability**: Users can scale services to fit their needs, customize applications, and access cloud services from anywhere with an internet connection.
2. **Flexibility**: Cloud services offer a lot of flexibility in terms of operating systems, programming languages, and the underlying architecture.
3. **Pay-as-you-go Model**: This pricing model means users only pay for the services they use, which helps companies save money and scale up or down quickly as their needs change.

Impact on Businesses and IT Infrastructure

The advent of cloud computing has had profound implications for businesses and IT infrastructure:

- **Cost Efficiency**: Companies can reduce costs related to acquiring, maintaining, and upgrading physical hardware and software.
- **Business Agility**: Cloud computing allows businesses to respond more quickly to market changes, with the ability to rapidly deploy new applications or scale existing ones.

- **Innovation and Collaboration**: It has enabled a new level of innovation and collaboration, making it easier to share data and work together in real-time, regardless of location.

From Simple Storage to Complex Solutions

Cloud services have evolved from simple data storage solutions to complex enterprise applications and platforms. Today, cloud providers offer a range of services including Software as a Service (SaaS), Platform as a Service (PaaS), and Infrastructure as a Service (IaaS), catering to a myriad of computing needs.

Conclusion

The evolution of cloud computing is a testament to the rapid advancements in technology and a reflection of the growing need for more flexible, cost-effective, and scalable computing solutions. As cloud computing continues to evolve, it is reshaping the technological landscape, offering new possibilities and challenges for businesses and individuals alike.

1.3. Defining Hybrid Cloud: Integration of Mainframes and Cloud Services

The concept of the hybrid cloud represents a significant advancement in the field of computing, offering a balanced and integrated approach that combines the strengths of different computing environments. It's particularly relevant in the context of integrating traditional mainframes with modern cloud services.

Definition of Hybrid Cloud

A hybrid cloud is an IT architecture that incorporates a mix of on-premises data centers (often including mainframes), private cloud services, and public cloud services, with orchestration between these platforms. This model offers flexibility and more deployment options, enabling businesses to optimize their existing infrastructure, security, and compliance.

Integration of Mainframes into Hybrid Cloud

The integration of mainframes into a hybrid cloud environment is a strategic approach that brings together the best of both worlds:

1. **Leveraging Mainframe Strengths**: Mainframes are renowned for their high-speed processing capabilities, robust security, and reliability, especially in handling large-scale transaction processing. These features make them indispensable for certain critical business operations.

2. **Utilizing Cloud Flexibility**: Cloud services, on the other hand, offer scalability, cost-efficiency, and innovation. They provide the agility to quickly deploy new services and the capability to process and analyze vast amounts of data.

The Role of Mainframes in a Hybrid Cloud Model

In the hybrid cloud model, mainframes often continue to serve as the backbone for core, mission-critical applications. This includes roles such as:

- Processing high-volume transactions in sectors like banking and finance.
- Managing large databases and complex ERP systems.
- Serving as a secure repository for sensitive data.

Interfacing with Cloud-Based Applications

While mainframes handle critical tasks, cloud-based applications and services offer complementary functionalities:

- **Customer Relationship Management (CRM) and Analytics**: These services are typically more adaptable and scalable when hosted on cloud platforms, providing valuable insights and enhanced customer engagement tools.
- **Development and Test Environments**: The cloud offers an ideal environment for development and testing, providing flexibility and reducing the time and cost associated with these activities.

Benefits of a Hybrid Cloud Approach

1. **Modernization Without Overhaul**: Organizations can modernize their IT infrastructure without completely

replacing their existing mainframe systems, protecting substantial investments and leveraging proven technologies.

2. **Seamless Data Exchange**: Hybrid cloud environments enable seamless data exchange and integration between mainframe and cloud-based applications, improving efficiency and enabling more advanced data analytics.
3. **Workload Balancing**: With a hybrid cloud, workloads can be dynamically allocated between mainframes and cloud resources, optimizing performance and cost.
4. **Expanded Functionality**: The combination of mainframe and cloud technologies allows organizations to expand their capabilities, adopting new cloud-based services and innovations while maintaining their robust mainframe operations.

Conclusion

In essence, the hybrid cloud model symbolizes a bridge between the traditional and the modern, merging the reliable and powerful capabilities of mainframes with the dynamic and scalable nature of cloud computing. This integration allows organizations to create a more agile, efficient, and future-proof IT infrastructure, capable of meeting the diverse and evolving demands of the digital era.

Chapter 2: The Architecture of Mainframes in a Hybrid Cloud Setup

The integration of mainframes with hybrid cloud architecture represents a confluence of traditional and modern IT environments. This chapter delves into the architectural aspects of this integration, highlighting how the robustness of mainframes can be synergistically combined with the versatility of cloud computing.

Core Components of Modern Mainframes

Modern mainframes have evolved significantly from their early predecessors, incorporating advanced technologies while maintaining their hallmark characteristics of reliability, security, and scalability. Key components include:

1. **Central Processing Unit (CPU)**: Modern mainframes use powerful, multi-core CPUs designed for high-volume, high-speed processing tasks.
2. **Storage**: They employ large-scale, high-speed storage systems, capable of handling massive amounts of data with quick access times.
3. **Memory**: High-capacity, fast-access memory is critical for efficient processing of large datasets and complex

applications.
4. **I/O Systems**: Advanced Input/Output systems in mainframes are designed to handle a vast number of simultaneous transactions and data transfers.
5. **Operating Systems**: Mainframes run on specialized operating systems (like z/OS for IBM mainframes) that are optimized for their hardware and workload characteristics.
6. **Security Features**: They include advanced encryption capabilities and robust security protocols to protect sensitive data and transactions.

Hybrid Cloud Architecture: Combining Mainframes and Cloud Infrastructure

Hybrid cloud architecture in the context of mainframes involves the integration of these robust systems with cloud environments. This architecture typically includes:

1. **On-Premises Mainframes**: Serving as the powerhouse for processing high-volume transactions and managing critical data.
2. **Private Clouds**: Often hosted on-premises or in a controlled environment, private clouds offer a secure and customizable cloud solution.
3. **Public Clouds**: Services like AWS, Azure, or Google Cloud provide scalable and flexible resources for various applications.
4. **Connectivity and Integration Tools**: Essential for seamless communication between mainframe and cloud environments. This includes APIs, middleware, and network configurations that enable data and application interoperability.
5. **Management and Orchestration Layers**: These layers provide unified control and visibility across the hybrid

environment, enabling efficient management of resources and workloads.

Mainframe Integration with Public and Private Clouds

Integrating mainframes with both public and private clouds involves several key considerations:

1. **Data Integration**: Ensuring smooth and secure data flow between mainframes and cloud platforms. This may involve data replication, synchronization, or using data gateways.
2. **Application Integration**: Leveraging modern application development approaches, such as microservices and containerization, to integrate mainframe applications with cloud-native services.
3. **Network Integration**: Establishing robust and secure network connections between mainframes and cloud environments, ensuring reliable and fast data transfer.
4. **Security and Compliance**: Implementing consistent security policies and compliance measures across the hybrid environment, addressing the diverse security models of mainframes and cloud services.
5. **Workload Management**: Strategically distributing workloads between mainframe and cloud resources based on factors like cost, performance, and business priorities.

Conclusion

The architecture of mainframes in a hybrid cloud setup represents a complex yet strategically advantageous IT landscape. It leverages the unparalleled processing power and security of mainframes, combined with the scalability, flexibility, and innovation of cloud computing. This architecture not only enhances the capabilities of traditional IT systems but also paves the way for new levels of efficiency, agility, and growth in the digital age.

2.1. Core Components of Modern Mainframes

Modern mainframes are marvels of engineering, combining cutting-edge technology with the robustness and reliability that have been their hallmark for decades. These systems are designed to meet the most demanding business requirements, offering unparalleled performance in handling vast amounts of data and transactions. The core components of modern mainframes reflect their evolution and their continued relevance in today's technology landscape.

1. Central Processing Unit (CPU)

- **Multi-core CPUs**: Modern mainframes use sophisticated, multi-core processors that can handle an immense volume of transactions and computational tasks. These CPUs are specifically designed for high-throughput, ensuring that mainframes can process complex operations quickly and efficiently.
- **Parallel Processing**: Many modern mainframe CPUs are capable of parallel processing, allowing them to execute multiple instructions simultaneously, further enhancing their performance capabilities.

2. Storage

- **High-Speed Storage Systems**: Modern mainframes are equipped with large-scale storage systems that provide quick access times, essential for processing large datasets and enabling real-time data analytics.
- **Storage Technology**: These systems often use advanced storage technologies like solid-state drives (SSDs) and high-speed disk arrays, offering faster data retrieval and improved reliability compared to traditional hard drives.

3. Memory

- **High-Capacity Memory**: The memory in modern mainframes is designed for speed and capacity, crucial for handling large-scale applications and data-intensive processes.
- **Efficient Data Handling**: Fast-access memory enables efficient processing of large datasets, reducing latency and improving overall system performance.

4. I/O Systems

- **Handling High Volume Transactions**: The Input/Output systems in mainframes are engineered to manage a vast number of simultaneous transactions, a critical feature for sectors like banking and telecommunications.
- **Advanced I/O Technologies**: These systems often incorporate cutting-edge I/O technologies that ensure efficient data transfer and communication with other systems and peripherals.

5. Operating Systems

- **Specialized Operating Systems**: Mainframes run on operating systems that are tailored to their specific hardware architecture. For example, IBM mainframes typically operate on z/OS, which is known for its robustness and ability to handle complex, high-volume workloads.
- **Optimization for Workloads**: These operating systems are optimized for the unique workload characteristics of mainframes, ensuring efficient utilization of system resources.

6. Security Features

- **Advanced Encryption**: Modern mainframes include sophisticated encryption capabilities to protect sensitive data, crucial for industries that handle confidential information.
- **Robust Security Protocols**: They employ stringent security protocols and mechanisms, ensuring the integrity and security of data and transactions.

Conclusion

The core components of modern mainframes exemplify the blend of tradition and innovation. While they retain the fundamental attributes of reliability, security, and scalability, they also incorporate the latest technological advancements. This makes them not only relevant but indispensable in today's fast-paced, data-driven world, where processing power, data security, and system reliability are more critical than ever.

2.2. Hybrid Cloud Architecture: Combining Mainframes and Cloud Infrastructure

Hybrid cloud architecture, especially when it involves the integration of mainframes, represents a strategic melding of traditional and modern IT infrastructures. This architecture leverages the strengths of both environments to create a versatile, robust, and scalable computing platform. Let's delve into the key components of this architecture:

1. On-Premises Mainframes

- **Role as Powerhouses**: In this setup, mainframes continue to serve their traditional role as powerhouses for processing high-volume transactions and managing critical data. They are especially valuable in industries like finance, healthcare, and government, where processing speed and data integrity are paramount.
- **Integration with Hybrid Cloud**: The mainframe's role in a hybrid cloud architecture is to provide a reliable and secure base for core business functions, while other aspects of the business leverage cloud flexibility.

2. Private Clouds

- **Customizable and Secure**: Private clouds are cloud environments dedicated solely to one organization. They can be hosted on-premises or in a data center controlled by the organization. These clouds offer enhanced security and control, making them suitable for sensitive data and critical applications.
- **Complementing Mainframes**: In a hybrid cloud architecture, private clouds often handle workloads that require more flexibility than mainframes can provide, but still need the security and control that a private environment offers.

3. Public Clouds

- **Scalability and Flexibility**: Public cloud services, provided by companies like Amazon Web Services (AWS), Microsoft Azure, or Google Cloud, offer resources that are scalable and flexible. They are ideal for workloads that have variable demands, such as web applications, development projects, and big data analytics.
- **Integration with Mainframes**: Public clouds complement mainframes by providing additional resources that can be quickly scaled up or down as needed, allowing organizations to respond agilely to changing business needs.

4. Connectivity and Integration Tools

- **Seamless Communication**: Tools for integration and connectivity are vital for ensuring that mainframes and cloud environments (both private and public) communicate seamlessly. This includes utilizing APIs (Application Programming Interfaces), middleware, and specific network configurations.

- **Data and Application Interoperability**: These tools and technologies enable the smooth transfer of data and the interoperability of applications across the different environments, ensuring that the hybrid cloud functions as a cohesive unit.

5. Management and Orchestration Layers

- **Unified Control and Visibility**: Management and orchestration layers in hybrid cloud architecture are crucial for providing oversight and control across the diverse environments. This includes tools for monitoring, managing workloads, and ensuring security across the system.
- **Efficient Resource Management**: These layers help in efficiently managing resources and workloads, ensuring that they are allocated to the most appropriate environment (mainframe, private cloud, or public cloud) based on specific requirements like performance, cost, and compliance.

Conclusion

Hybrid cloud architecture involving mainframes is a testament to the evolving nature of IT infrastructure. It brings together the reliability and power of mainframes with the agility and innovation of cloud computing. This architectural approach allows organizations to harness the best of both worlds, providing a flexible, scalable, and secure environment that can meet the varied and dynamic needs of modern businesses.

2.3. Mainframe Integration with Public and Private Clouds

Integrating mainframes with public and private clouds is a complex but strategically beneficial undertaking that involves a series of nuanced considerations. This integration allows organizations to leverage the unique strengths of each environment, leading to improved efficiency, agility, and innovation. Let's explore these key considerations in detail:

1. Data Integration

- **Smooth and Secure Data Flow**: Ensuring a seamless and secure data exchange between mainframes and cloud platforms is crucial. This involves managing data consistency, availability, and integrity across different environments.
- **Replication and Synchronization**: Techniques like data replication and synchronization are often employed to maintain data consistency. This may also involve real-time data streaming or batch processing, depending on the application requirements.
- **Data Gateways:** Data gateways and other middleware solutions can facilitate this integration, acting as bridges that translate and transfer data between mainframes and

cloud environments.

2. Application Integration

- **Modern Development Approaches**: Integrating mainframe applications with cloud-native services often requires adopting modern application development methodologies like microservices architecture and containerization.
- **Microservices and Containerization**: These approaches allow mainframe applications to be broken down into smaller, more manageable pieces that can interact more easily with cloud-based services.
- **APIs and Service Mesh**: APIs (Application Programming Interfaces) and service mesh architectures are also key to this integration, enabling different applications to communicate and work together effectively.

3. Network Integration

- **Robust and Secure Network Connections**: Establishing strong and secure network connections is essential for the reliable and fast transfer of data between mainframes and cloud environments.
- **VPN and Direct Connect Solutions**: Solutions like Virtual Private Networks (VPNs) or direct connect services (such as AWS Direct Connect or Azure ExpressRoute) can be used to establish secure and reliable connections.
- **Network Performance and Reliability**: Attention must be paid to network latency, bandwidth requirements, and overall network performance to ensure that the integration

does not hinder operational efficiency.

4. Security and Compliance

- **Consistent Security Policies**: Implementing uniform security policies across the hybrid environment is critical. This involves understanding and addressing the different security models and capabilities of mainframes and cloud services.
- **Regulatory Compliance**: Compliance with industry standards and regulations must be maintained across all environments. This may involve data encryption, access controls, and regular security audits.
- **Shared Responsibility Model**: In public cloud scenarios, understanding the shared responsibility model – where cloud providers and users share security and compliance responsibilities – is vital.

5. Workload Management

- **Strategic Distribution of Workloads**: Effective workload management involves strategically distributing tasks and applications between mainframe and cloud resources. This is based on various factors like cost, performance requirements, and business priorities.
- **Dynamic Resource Allocation**: Tools and strategies for dynamic resource allocation and scaling can help optimize workload distribution, ensuring that each environment is used for tasks where it excels.
- **Monitoring and Analytics**: Continuous monitoring and analytics are essential for understanding workload patterns and making informed decisions about resource allocation.

Conclusion

The integration of mainframes with public and private clouds is a multidimensional process that requires careful planning and execution. It involves ensuring smooth data and application integration, establishing robust network connections, maintaining stringent security and compliance standards, and managing workloads effectively. When done correctly, this integration allows organizations to harness the combined power of mainframe reliability and cloud flexibility, leading to a more resilient, agile, and efficient IT infrastructure.

Chapter 3: Managing Data in Mainframes and Hybrid Cloud Systems

Data management in environments that combine mainframes and hybrid cloud systems is a critical aspect of modern IT infrastructure. This chapter explores the intricacies of data storage and management within these complex environments, focusing on compatibility, integrity, and security.

Data Storage and Management in Mainframes

- **High-Volume, High-Speed Processing**: Mainframes are designed for high-volume data processing, making them ideal for industries where large-scale transaction processing is critical.
- **Hierarchical Storage Management (HSM)**: Mainframes often employ HSM systems, which automatically move data between high-speed disks and slower storage media based on the frequency of access, optimizing performance and storage efficiency.
- **Database Management Systems (DBMS)**: Mainframes commonly use powerful DBMS for managing large datasets. These systems are optimized for the unique architecture of mainframes, ensuring efficient data

handling and retrieval.

Cloud Storage Solutions: Compatibility with Mainframe Data

- **Integration Challenges**: One of the key challenges in integrating mainframe and cloud storage solutions is ensuring compatibility between different data formats and protocols.
- **Data Transformation and Migration Tools**: Tools and services are often used to transform mainframe data into formats suitable for cloud storage. This can include ETL (Extract, Transform, Load) processes, data pipelines, and APIs.
- **Hybrid Cloud Storage Options**: Cloud storage solutions, like object storage, block storage, and file storage, offer different benefits and are selected based on the specific needs of the application or workload. Ensuring that these solutions are compatible with mainframe data is crucial for seamless integration.

Ensuring Data Integrity and Security in a Hybrid Environment

- **Data Integrity**: Maintaining data integrity across mainframes and cloud systems is crucial. This involves ensuring that data remains accurate, consistent, and reliable as it moves between different environments.
- **Encryption and Data Masking**: Techniques like encryption and data masking are used to secure data both at rest and in transit. Encryption is especially important when transferring data between mainframes and cloud environments.
- **Access Control and Authentication**: Implementing

robust access control and authentication mechanisms ensures that only authorized users can access sensitive data. This is critical in a hybrid environment where multiple systems interact.

- **Compliance and Regulatory Requirements**: Adhering to compliance and regulatory requirements is a key consideration, especially in industries like finance and healthcare. This involves implementing data governance policies and regular audits.
- **Disaster Recovery and Data Backup**: Ensuring robust disaster recovery and data backup strategies is vital. This includes leveraging cloud resources for backups and implementing failover mechanisms for critical mainframe applications.

Conclusion

Managing data in mainframes and hybrid cloud systems requires a careful approach that balances the strengths and limitations of each environment. It involves not only technical integration and compatibility considerations but also a strong focus on maintaining data integrity and security. By effectively addressing these challenges, organizations can ensure that their data remains a valuable asset that drives business decisions and operations, regardless of where it resides.

3.1. Data Storage and Management in Mainframes

Data storage and management in mainframes are fundamental aspects that underscore their enduring relevance in modern computing environments, especially in scenarios demanding high-volume, high-speed processing. Let's delve into these key features:

High-Volume, High-Speed Processing

- **Designed for Transactional Workloads**: Mainframes are inherently designed to handle large-scale transaction processing. This is a critical feature for industries like banking, finance, insurance, and retail, where processing large numbers of transactions accurately and quickly is essential.
- **Optimized for Performance**: The hardware and software of mainframes are optimized to ensure high throughput and minimal latency in data processing. This capability is vital for applications where performance and response time are crucial.

Hierarchical Storage Management (HSM)

- **Automated Data Management**: Hierarchical Storage

Management in mainframes is a sophisticated approach to managing storage resources. HSM systems automatically manage the placement of data across various storage media – from high-speed SSDs to slower, more economical storage options like magnetic tape or older disk drives.

- **Performance and Efficiency**: By moving less frequently accessed data to slower storage and keeping frequently accessed data on faster storage, HSM optimizes both performance and storage costs. This approach is particularly beneficial for managing large volumes of data over long periods.

Database Management Systems (DBMS)

- **Handling Large Datasets**: Mainframes commonly use robust DBMS that are capable of managing and manipulating vast amounts of data. These databases are a cornerstone in environments where data integrity and availability are paramount.
- **Optimization for Mainframe Architecture**: The DBMS used in mainframes are specifically optimized for their unique architecture. This includes special optimizations for data storage formats, indexing techniques, and query processing, ensuring efficient handling and retrieval of data.
- **Advanced Features**: Modern mainframe DBMS offer advanced features like real-time analytics, high availability, and strong transactional integrity, making them ideal for critical business applications.

Conclusion

In summary, the capabilities of mainframes in data storage and management are a testament to their design and technological evolution. They are not only equipped to handle the high-speed processing of massive volumes of transactions but also ensure efficient and cost-effective storage management through HSM. Additionally, the use of specialized DBMS optimized for mainframe architecture further enhances their ability to manage large datasets effectively. These features collectively make mainframes an indispensable asset in data-intensive industries and applications.

High-Volume, High-Speed Processing

High-volume, high-speed processing is a hallmark characteristic of mainframes, making them indispensable in environments where handling large-scale transactional workloads is crucial. Let's explore these aspects in more detail:

Designed for Transactional Workloads

- **Core to Industry Operations**: In sectors such as banking, finance, insurance, and retail, mainframes are central to operations. These industries require the processing of millions of transactions daily, from financial transfers to insurance claims and retail purchases.
- **Accuracy and Speed**: The ability of mainframes to process these transactions both accurately and rapidly is vital. Any delay or error can have significant repercussions, affecting customer satisfaction, financial integrity, and regulatory compliance.
- **Scalability**: Mainframes can handle increasing transaction volumes without proportional increases in complexity or resource consumption. This scalability is essential for industries that experience variable transaction volumes, such as retail sectors during peak shopping seasons.

Optimized for Performance

- **Hardware Superiority**: Mainframe hardware is specifically designed for high-throughput data processing. This includes powerful processors, extensive memory, and fast I/O (Input/Output) capabilities. Such hardware configurations enable mainframes to handle substantial transaction loads with ease.
- **Software Efficiency**: The software running on

mainframes, including operating systems and transaction processing systems, is optimized for these tasks. This software is designed to maximize throughput, manage large volumes of concurrent transactions, and minimize response times.

- **Minimal Latency**: In transaction processing, latency is a critical concern. Mainframes excel in maintaining minimal latency, ensuring that transaction processing is not only fast but also consistent, providing predictable performance even under heavy load.
- **Reliability and Uptime**: Mainframes are renowned for their reliability and high uptime. This is crucial in industries where even a brief downtime can result in significant operational disruptions and financial losses.

Conclusion

In summary, the design and optimization of mainframes for high-volume, high-speed transaction processing make them an integral component of many critical industry operations. Their hardware and software are fine-tuned to deliver exceptional performance, scalability, and reliability, ensuring that they can meet the demanding requirements of processing large numbers of transactions swiftly and accurately. This capability underpins the continued reliance on mainframe technology in various sectors, despite the advent of newer computing paradigms.

Hierarchical Storage Management (HSM)

Hierarchical Storage Management (HSM) in mainframes is a critical component for efficient data management, especially in environments dealing with vast amounts of data. It represents a strategic approach to managing storage resources that balances performance needs with cost considerations. Let's delve into the key aspects of HSM:

Automated Data Management

- **Dynamic Data Placement**: HSM systems in mainframes are designed to automatically manage the placement and movement of data across various storage media. This process is typically based on the usage patterns and access frequency of the data.
- **Range of Storage Media**: The storage hierarchy in an HSM system can range from high-speed Solid State Drives (SSDs) for frequently accessed data to slower, more cost-effective options like magnetic tape or traditional hard disk drives for less frequently accessed information.
- **Intelligent Allocation**: The system intelligently allocates data to the appropriate storage tier. For instance, data that is accessed frequently and requires quick retrieval will be kept on faster, more expensive storage media, while older, less frequently accessed data is moved to slower, cheaper storage.

Performance and Efficiency

- **Optimizing Access and Cost**: The primary goal of HSM is to optimize the balance between access speed and storage cost. By ensuring that frequently accessed data is readily available on faster storage mediums, HSM systems improve overall system performance.

- **Efficient Use of Resources**: By relegating less frequently accessed data to more economical storage options, HSM makes efficient use of storage resources, reducing costs without significantly impacting data accessibility.
- **Long-Term Data Management**: This approach is particularly beneficial for managing large volumes of data over extended periods. It allows for effective long-term data storage strategies, essential for organizations that need to retain data for compliance, historical analysis, or backup purposes.
- **Automated Lifecycle Management**: HSM often includes automated data lifecycle management policies, where data is automatically moved through different storage tiers based on its age, usage, or other predefined criteria.

Conclusion

In summary, Hierarchical Storage Management in mainframes is a sophisticated and automated approach to data storage that plays a crucial role in large-scale data environments. By intelligently managing the placement of data across a hierarchy of storage solutions, HSM systems optimize both the performance and the cost-efficiency of data storage. This technology is particularly advantageous for organizations that deal with large data volumes and require a strategic approach to long-term data management.

Database Management Systems (DBMS)

Database Management Systems (DBMS) in mainframes are pivotal for managing large datasets, ensuring data integrity and availability, and providing advanced functionalities tailored for critical business applications. Here's a detailed look at these aspects:

Handling Large Datasets

- **Robust Data Management**: Mainframes utilize powerful DBMS that are engineered to handle, manage, and manipulate vast quantities of data. This capability is crucial in sectors like finance, healthcare, and government, where managing large databases is a routine requirement.
- **Data Integrity and Availability**: These DBMS ensure high levels of data integrity and availability. This means data remains accurate, consistent, and accessible when needed, which is essential for operations that rely on precision and reliability in data handling.

Optimization for Mainframe Architecture

- **Tailored for Mainframe Systems**: The DBMS used in mainframes are specifically optimized to take full advantage of their hardware and architectural strengths. This ensures that the systems are not just capable of storing large amounts of data but can do so efficiently.
- **Efficient Data Storage and Retrieval**: Optimizations include specific data storage formats, indexing techniques, and advanced query processing capabilities. These optimizations ensure that data handling and retrieval are both efficient and effective, minimizing latency and maximizing throughput.
- **Resource Optimization**: Mainframe DBMS are designed

to optimize the use of system resources, such as CPU cycles and memory, ensuring that the system can handle multiple high-volume tasks simultaneously without degradation in performance.

Advanced Features

- **Real-Time Analytics**: Modern mainframe DBMS are equipped with capabilities for real-time analytics. This allows for immediate data processing and analysis, which is vital for decision-making processes in fast-paced business environments.
- **High Availability**: They offer high availability features, ensuring that the database services are always up and running, which is crucial for applications where downtime can have significant business implications.
- **Transactional Integrity**: These systems provide strong transactional integrity, meaning that all transactional processes are accurate, reliable, and consistent. This is particularly important in environments where transactional accuracy is non-negotiable, such as in banking and financial services.
- **Security Features**: Enhanced security features are also a key component of these DBMS, providing robust mechanisms to protect sensitive data from unauthorized access or breaches.

Conclusion

In summary, the DBMS in mainframes are more than just data repositories; they are sophisticated systems optimized for handling large datasets with high efficiency, ensuring data integrity, and providing advanced functionalities. These features make them ideal for critical business applications that not only demand large-scale data processing capabilities but also require these processes to be reliable, secure, and readily available. The advanced capabilities of modern mainframe DBMS, like real-time analytics and high availability, further extend their utility in today's fast-paced business world.

3.2. Cloud Storage Solutions: Compatibility with Mainframe Data

Integrating mainframe data with cloud storage solutions is a crucial aspect of creating a cohesive hybrid cloud environment. This process, however, comes with its own set of challenges and requirements, especially regarding compatibility and data transformation. Here's an in-depth look at these aspects:

Integration Challenges

- **Data Format and Protocol Differences**: Mainframes typically use data formats and communication protocols that differ significantly from those used in modern cloud environments. This disparity can create challenges in ensuring seamless data exchange and integration.
- **Legacy Systems Compatibility**: Many mainframes run legacy systems with data stored in older formats that may not be directly compatible with newer cloud-based storage solutions.
- **Performance Considerations**: Ensuring that the integration does not negatively impact the performance of both mainframe and cloud environments is also a critical challenge.

Data Transformation and Migration Tools

- **ETL Processes**: Extract, Transform, Load (ETL) processes are commonly used to migrate data from mainframes to cloud environments. ETL involves extracting data from the mainframe, transforming it into a format suitable for cloud storage, and then loading it into the cloud system.
- **Data Pipelines**: Creating data pipelines can automate the process of moving and transforming data, making the integration process more efficient and less prone to errors.
- **APIs for Integration**: Application Programming Interfaces (APIs) play a crucial role in this integration, allowing different systems to communicate and share data despite differences in underlying technologies.
- **Middleware Solutions**: Middleware can act as a bridge between mainframe and cloud environments, facilitating data translation, transformation, and transfer.

Hybrid Cloud Storage Options

- **Object Storage**: This is ideal for unstructured data and is highly scalable. It's suitable for data that doesn't require frequent changes, such as backup files, multimedia content, and archival data.
- **Block Storage**: Block storage is often used for structured data that requires frequent reading and writing operations. It's commonly employed for database storage and applications that need high-performance storage solutions.
- **File Storage**: This is used for data that needs to be accessed and managed as files and is a good option for shared storage scenarios, such as documents and media files.
- **Compatibility Considerations**: When integrating

mainframe data with these cloud storage options, it's crucial to consider compatibility. This includes ensuring data is in the right format and that the storage solution can meet the performance and access requirements of the mainframe applications.

Conclusion

Integrating cloud storage solutions with mainframe data is a complex process that requires careful consideration of data formats, compatibility, and the appropriate use of transformation and migration tools. The choice of cloud storage - whether object, block, or file storage - should align with the specific needs of the applications and workloads involved. Successfully addressing these challenges can lead to a more flexible and scalable hybrid cloud environment, leveraging the strengths of both mainframe and cloud technologies.

Integration Challenges

Integrating mainframe systems with cloud environments presents a unique set of challenges, primarily due to differences in data formats, protocols, and the compatibility issues with legacy systems. Let's delve into these integration challenges in more detail:

Data Format and Protocol Differences

- **Inherent Disparities**: Mainframe systems often use proprietary or specialized data formats and communication protocols that have been in place for decades. These formats and protocols are typically quite different from the open or standardized formats commonly used in modern cloud environments.
- **Seamless Data Exchange**: The challenge lies in ensuring seamless data exchange and integration between these distinct systems. Data from mainframes may need to be converted or reformatted before it can be used or stored in cloud environments.
- **Middleware and Bridging Technologies**: Often, middleware solutions or bridging technologies are required to facilitate this conversion and enable communication between the mainframe and cloud systems.

Legacy Systems Compatibility

- **Older Data Formats**: Many mainframes run on legacy systems that store data in formats which are no longer widely used or supported. This can pose significant challenges when integrating with cloud-based systems that are optimized for modern data formats.
- **Data Transformation Needs**: To address this, data often needs to be transformed into a format that is compatible

with cloud storage solutions, which can be a complex and resource-intensive process.

- **Preserving Data Integrity**: It's crucial to ensure that this transformation process preserves the integrity and accuracy of the data, especially when dealing with critical business information.

Performance Considerations

- **Balancing Performance**: One of the primary concerns in integrating mainframes with cloud environments is maintaining the performance levels of both systems. The integration should not result in degraded performance in either the mainframe or the cloud environment.
- **Optimized Data Transfer**: Efficient and optimized data transfer mechanisms need to be in place to minimize latency and ensure that the data is available when and where it's needed.
- **Resource Allocation**: Adequate resources must be allocated to handle the additional load that data integration may place on both the mainframe and cloud systems. This involves careful planning and potentially scaling up resources to meet the demands of the integrated environment.

Conclusion

Integrating mainframe systems with cloud environments is a complex endeavor that requires careful consideration of data formats, legacy system compatibility, and performance impacts. The key to successful integration lies in effectively bridging the gap between old and new technologies, ensuring seamless data exchange, and maintaining the performance and integrity of both systems. By addressing these challenges, organizations can leverage the combined strengths of mainframes and cloud computing to create a powerful, integrated IT infrastructure.

Data Transformation and Migration Tools

Data transformation and migration tools are essential in bridging the gap between mainframe and cloud environments. These tools and processes facilitate the movement and integration of data, ensuring compatibility and maintaining integrity. Let's explore these tools in more detail:

ETL Processes

- **Extraction**: The first step involves extracting data from the mainframe environment. This step is crucial as it involves pulling out the necessary data without impacting the performance of the mainframe system.
- **Transformation**: Once extracted, the data often needs to be transformed. This could involve converting the data into a different format, cleansing the data, or restructuring it to fit the schema used in the cloud environment.
- **Loading**: The final step is loading the transformed data into the cloud system. This needs to be done in a way that ensures data integrity and efficiency.

Data Pipelines

- **Automation of Data Movement**: Data pipelines automate the process of moving data from mainframes to the cloud. They can continuously move data in real-time or at scheduled intervals.
- **Reducing Errors**: Automation through data pipelines can significantly reduce the chances of errors that are common in manual data transfer processes.
- **Streamlining Integration**: By using data pipelines, the process of integrating mainframe data with cloud environments becomes more streamlined and manageable.

APIs for Integration

- **Facilitating Communication**: APIs are crucial in enabling communication between the mainframe and cloud environments. They provide a set of protocols and tools for building software and applications that can access the features or data of an operating system, application, or other services.
- **Bridging Technology Gaps**: APIs help in bridging the technology gaps between mainframe and cloud systems, allowing them to communicate effectively despite differences in underlying technologies.

Middleware Solutions

- **Acting as Intermediaries**: Middleware solutions act as intermediaries between mainframe and cloud environments. They can handle the complexities of data translation and transformation.
- **Data Synchronization**: Middleware can ensure that data remains synchronized between the two environments, providing consistency and integrity.
- **Seamless Data Transfer**: These solutions can facilitate seamless data transfer, making it easier for organizations to integrate their existing mainframe systems with newer cloud technologies.

Conclusion

The use of data transformation and migration tools like ETL processes, data pipelines, APIs, and middleware is crucial in successfully integrating mainframe systems with cloud environments. These tools not only enable efficient and error-free data transfer but also ensure that the data remains consistent and usable across both platforms. By effectively leveraging these tools, organizations can create a cohesive and integrated IT infrastructure that combines the reliability and power of mainframes with the flexibility and scalability of cloud computing.

Hybrid Cloud Storage Options

Hybrid cloud storage options provide a range of solutions to accommodate different types of data and usage scenarios. Each storage type has its own set of characteristics, making it suitable for specific needs. Understanding these options is crucial when integrating mainframe data into a hybrid cloud environment. Let's examine these storage options and the compatibility considerations:

Object Storage

- **Ideal for Unstructured Data**: Object storage is designed to store large amounts of unstructured data. This includes data like videos, images, and backup files.
- **High Scalability**: One of the key advantages of object storage is its scalability. It can store vast amounts of data and is easily expandable.
- **Use Cases**: Common use cases include storing backup files, multimedia content, and archival data. It's particularly useful for data that does not require frequent updates or modifications.

Block Storage

- **Structured Data Storage**: Block storage is suitable for structured data that requires frequent read and write operations. It operates by storing data in fixed-sized blocks.
- **High Performance**: It is known for its high performance and is often used for applications that require fast, efficient, and reliable access to data.
- **Database Storage**: This makes block storage a preferred option for database storage and critical business applications that demand consistent performance and low-latency access.

File Storage

- **File-Based Access**: File storage allows data to be stored in a hierarchical structure. It's used for data that needs to be accessed and managed as files.
- **Shared Storage Scenarios**: It is well-suited for shared storage scenarios where multiple users need to access and manage data, such as in document storage and media libraries.
- **Familiar Structure**: The hierarchical structure of file storage is familiar and easy to navigate, making it a user-friendly option for managing shared data.

Compatibility Considerations

- **Data Format Compatibility**: When integrating mainframe data with cloud storage options, it's essential to ensure that the data is in a compatible format. This may require transforming mainframe data into formats that are suitable for object, block, or file storage.
- **Performance and Access Requirements**: The chosen storage solution should align with the performance and access requirements of the mainframe applications. For instance, applications that require high-speed access to data may be better served by block storage.
- **Integration Tools and Technologies**: Utilizing the appropriate integration tools and technologies is crucial for a smooth transition of data from mainframes to cloud storage. This includes middleware, APIs, and data transformation tools.
- **Ensuring Data Integrity**: In the process of integrating and migrating data, maintaining the integrity and consistency

of data is paramount. This is particularly important when dealing with critical business data stored on mainframes.

Conclusion

Choosing the right hybrid cloud storage option depends on the specific needs of the data and applications involved. Object storage, block storage, and file storage each offer unique advantages and are suitable for different scenarios. In integrating these with mainframe systems, compatibility, performance, and data integrity are key considerations that must be carefully addressed to ensure a successful hybrid cloud storage strategy.

3.3. Ensuring Data Integrity and Security in a Hybrid Environment

Ensuring data integrity and security in a hybrid environment, where mainframes and cloud systems coexist, is paramount. This challenge involves not only safeguarding data against unauthorized access or breaches but also ensuring its accuracy and consistency across diverse platforms. Let's explore the strategies and practices that are crucial in maintaining data integrity and security in such environments:

Data Integrity

- **Accuracy and Consistency**: It's essential to ensure that data remains accurate, consistent, and reliable as it moves between mainframe and cloud environments. This involves maintaining the integrity of the data during transfer, storage, and processing.
- **Data Synchronization**: Proper synchronization mechanisms should be in place to ensure that data changes are consistently updated across all systems.
- **Data Validation and Quality Checks**: Regular data validation and quality checks are necessary to detect and correct any inconsistencies or errors that might occur.

Encryption and Data Masking

- **Securing Data at Rest and in Transit**: Encryption is critical for protecting data both at rest (when stored) and in transit (during transfer). This is especially important when data is moved between different environments, such as from mainframes to cloud storage.
- **Data Masking**: This technique is used to obscure specific data within a database so that sensitive information is hidden from unauthorized users. It's particularly useful in environments where data needs to be shared with third parties or for development purposes.

Access Control and Authentication

- **Robust Access Control**: Implementing strong access control mechanisms ensures that only authorized personnel have access to sensitive data. This includes managing permissions and roles effectively.
- **Authentication Protocols**: Strong authentication protocols, such as multi-factor authentication (MFA), are essential to verify the identity of users accessing the systems.

Compliance and Regulatory Requirements

- **Meeting Industry Standards**: Different industries often have specific compliance and regulatory requirements, particularly sectors like finance, healthcare, and government. It's crucial to adhere to these standards to avoid legal and financial penalties.
- **Data Governance Policies**: Implementing comprehensive

data governance policies and conducting regular audits help in maintaining compliance and ensuring that data is managed responsibly.

Disaster Recovery and Data Backup

- **Robust Backup Strategies**: Regular backups are essential to prevent data loss. Cloud resources can be effectively utilized for storing backup data.
- **Disaster Recovery Planning**: A well-defined disaster recovery plan ensures that there are procedures in place to recover data and restore system functionality in the event of a system failure, data breach, or natural disaster.
- **Failover Mechanisms**: Implementing failover mechanisms for critical mainframe applications ensures business continuity and minimal service interruption during outages.

Conclusion

Maintaining data integrity and security in a hybrid environment is a multifaceted challenge that requires a combination of technical solutions and stringent policies. Encryption, data masking, access control, adherence to compliance standards, and robust disaster recovery and backup strategies are key components of a comprehensive approach to safeguard data in such environments. By implementing these practices, organizations can ensure that their data remains secure, accurate, and reliable, irrespective of whether it resides on mainframes or in the cloud.

Data Integrity

Maintaining data integrity in a hybrid environment involving both mainframes and cloud systems is a crucial aspect of ensuring that data remains a reliable asset for decision-making and operations. This process involves several key practices:

Accuracy and Consistency

- **Maintaining Integrity Across Platforms**: As data moves between different environments like mainframes and cloud systems, it's vital to maintain its accuracy and consistency. This involves careful handling during transfer, storage, and processing to prevent data corruption or loss.
- **Change Management**: Effective change management processes are essential to ensure that any updates, deletions, or modifications to the data are accurately reflected across all systems. This helps maintain the consistency of data irrespective of its location.

Data Synchronization

- **Real-time or Scheduled Updates**: Implementing proper synchronization mechanisms is crucial to ensure that data is consistently updated across all systems. This can be achieved through real-time synchronization or scheduled updates, depending on the business requirements and technical capabilities.
- **Conflict Resolution**: In cases where data is updated concurrently in multiple systems, mechanisms must be in place for conflict resolution to maintain data integrity. This involves defining rules for how data conflicts are handled and resolved.

Data Validation and Quality Checks

- **Regular Validation Processes**: Regular data validation processes are necessary to verify the accuracy and integrity of the data. This can include checking for data completeness, accuracy, and adherence to predefined formats or standards.
- **Quality Assurance Protocols**: Implementing quality assurance protocols helps in early detection and correction of any data inconsistencies or errors. This might involve automated checks, audits, and manual reviews.
- **Data Cleansing**: Periodic data cleansing routines can be established to identify and correct errors like duplications, incorrect entries, or outdated information. This is especially important in dynamic environments where data is frequently updated or changed.

Conclusion

Ensuring data integrity in a hybrid mainframe and cloud environment requires a comprehensive approach involving accurate and consistent data handling, effective synchronization mechanisms, and regular validation and quality checks. By implementing these practices, organizations can trust the reliability and accuracy of their data, which is essential for making informed decisions and maintaining efficient operations in a data-driven business landscape.

Encryption and Data Masking

Encryption and data masking are fundamental techniques in securing data, particularly in hybrid environments where data frequently moves between mainframes and cloud systems. These practices are essential for protecting sensitive information both at rest and in transit.

Encryption: Securing Data at Rest and in Transit

- **Encryption at Rest**: Encrypting data at rest involves converting data into a secure format when it's stored on a disk or storage medium. This is crucial for protecting data stored in mainframes, cloud storage, or any other data repositories from unauthorized access.
- **Encryption in Transit**: Encryption in transit is equally important as it secures data while it's being transferred between different systems or environments, such as from a mainframe to cloud storage. This protects data from being intercepted or tampered with during transmission.
- **Key Management**: Effective encryption strategies also involve robust key management practices. This includes secure generation, storage, and rotation of encryption keys to prevent unauthorized decryption.
- **End-to-End Encryption**: Implementing end-to-end encryption ensures that data is encrypted at its origin and decrypted only at its intended destination, reducing the risk of data exposure during transit.

Data Masking

- **Obscuring Sensitive Information**: Data masking involves obscuring specific data within a database so that the data remains usable for purposes like testing or analytics, but the sensitive information is concealed. This is done by altering or scrambling the data in a way that maintains its format and usability but removes its original value.

- **Use Cases**: This technique is particularly useful when sensitive data needs to be shared with third parties or external teams, such as in development environments or third-party testing scenarios. For example, a company might mask sensitive customer information before sharing a dataset with a software development contractor.
- **Dynamic and Static Masking**: Data masking can be static, where a copy of the data is masked and used, or dynamic, where masking rules are applied in real-time as the data is accessed, leaving the original data unchanged in the database.
- **Compliance with Privacy Regulations**: Data masking helps organizations comply with privacy laws and regulations, such as GDPR or HIPAA, by ensuring that sensitive data is not exposed to unauthorized personnel while still allowing for productive use of the data.

Conclusion

In a hybrid cloud and mainframe environment, encryption and data masking are essential for safeguarding data. Encryption protects the data's confidentiality, while data masking preserves its utility while protecting sensitive information. Together, these practices form a strong foundation for a comprehensive data security strategy, ensuring that sensitive information is protected throughout its lifecycle in the hybrid IT landscape.

Access Control and Authentication

Access control and authentication are crucial components in safeguarding sensitive data in a hybrid environment, where mainframe and cloud systems coexist. These security measures ensure that only authorized personnel can access critical data and systems, thereby protecting against unauthorized use and potential breaches.

Robust Access Control

- **Defining User Permissions**: Implementing a robust access control system involves defining and managing user permissions and roles effectively. This ensures that individuals can only access data and resources that are relevant to their role within the organization.
- **Role-Based Access Control (RBAC)**: RBAC is a common approach where access rights are assigned based on the roles of individual users within an organization. This simplifies the management of user permissions, making it easier to ensure that users have appropriate access levels.
- **Least Privilege Principle**: This principle dictates that users should be granted the minimum levels of access – or permissions – necessary to perform their job functions. This minimizes the risk of unauthorized access to sensitive data.
- **Regular Audits and Reviews**: Regular audits of access control lists and user permissions are essential to ensure that access rights remain appropriate over time, especially as roles and responsibilities within an organization change.

Authentication Protocols

- **Verifying User Identity**: Strong authentication protocols are crucial to verify the identity of users accessing the systems. This is especially important in hybrid environments where users may access systems remotely.
- **Multi-Factor Authentication (MFA)**: MFA requires users to provide two or more verification factors to gain access to a resource such as an application, online account, or a VPN. Common factors include something the user knows (like a password), something the user has (like a smartphone or a security token), and something the user is (like a fingerprint or other biometric verification).
- **Single Sign-On (SSO)**: SSO can be used to streamline the authentication process, particularly in environments where users require access to multiple systems or applications. It allows users to log in once and gain access to several systems without needing to authenticate again.
- **Adaptive Authentication**: This involves implementing additional security measures based on the context of the access request, such as the user's location, time of access, and type of data being accessed. Adaptive authentication can dynamically adjust the level of authentication required based on perceived risk.

Conclusion

Access control and authentication are vital for maintaining the security and integrity of data within a hybrid environment combining mainframe and cloud systems. Effective management of user permissions and roles, combined with strong authentication protocols, forms a critical line of defense against unauthorized access and potential security breaches. These security measures not only protect sensitive data but also help organizations comply with regulatory requirements and industry best practices.

Compliance and Regulatory Requirements

Compliance and regulatory requirements are critical aspects of data management and security, especially in a hybrid environment where mainframes and cloud systems coexist. Organizations in regulated industries such as finance, healthcare, and government are particularly affected. Let's delve into these crucial areas:

Meeting Industry Standards

- **Understanding Regulatory Landscape**: Different industries are subject to various regulatory standards that govern how data should be handled, stored, and protected. For instance, the finance industry often has to comply with regulations like the Sarbanes-Oxley Act (SOX), the healthcare sector with the Health Insurance Portability and Accountability Act (HIPAA), and all sectors handling European data with the General Data Protection Regulation (GDPR).
- **Avoiding Penalties**: Non-compliance with these regulations can result in significant legal and financial repercussions. Therefore, understanding and adhering to these standards is not just a matter of best practice but a legal necessity.
- **Tailored Compliance Strategies**: Compliance strategies should be tailored to meet the specific requirements of each regulation. This might include implementing specific security measures, maintaining particular data handling procedures, or conducting regular compliance training for employees.

Data Governance Policies

- **Establishing Data Governance Framework**:

Implementing comprehensive data governance policies involves establishing a framework that defines who has the authority and control over data assets and how these assets can be used. This framework should align with the relevant regulatory requirements.

- **Regular Audits and Assessments**: Regular audits and assessments are key to maintaining compliance. These should be conducted to ensure that data governance policies are being correctly followed and to identify any areas where improvements can be made.
- **Transparency and Accountability**: Data governance should promote transparency and accountability in data management practices. This includes maintaining clear records of data processing activities, data access logs, and changes to data policies.
- **Employee Training and Awareness**: Employees should be trained and made aware of the data governance policies and the importance of compliance. This helps in fostering a culture of compliance and responsibility across the organization.

Conclusion

Compliance and regulatory requirements are fundamental in managing data in a hybrid environment, particularly for organizations operating under stringent regulatory frameworks. Adhering to these requirements through tailored compliance strategies, comprehensive data governance policies, regular audits, and employee training is essential to avoid legal repercussions and to maintain the trust of clients, stakeholders, and regulatory bodies. This adherence not only ensures legal and ethical use of data but also plays a crucial role in protecting an organization's reputation and operational integrity.

Disaster Recovery and Data Backup

Disaster recovery and data backup are critical components of a comprehensive data management strategy, especially in hybrid environments combining mainframe and cloud systems. These measures are vital for ensuring business continuity and mitigating the risks associated with data loss and system failures.

Robust Backup Strategies

- **Regular Data Backups**: Conducting regular backups is a fundamental practice to safeguard data against loss. This includes periodic backups of critical data stored on mainframes and within cloud environments.
- **Utilizing Cloud Resources**: Cloud resources can be effectively used for data backups due to their scalability and flexibility. Cloud storage can serve as an off-site backup location, providing an additional layer of data protection.
- **Backup Testing**: Regular testing of backup processes is essential to ensure that data can be successfully restored when needed. This includes verifying that backups are complete, up-to-date, and can be restored within an acceptable time frame.

Disaster Recovery Planning

- **Comprehensive Disaster Recovery Plan**: A well-defined disaster recovery plan outlines procedures and steps to recover data and restore system functionality in the event of various disasters, including system failures, data breaches, or natural disasters.
- **Risk Assessment and Planning**: The plan should be based on a thorough risk assessment and include strategies to

address different types of potential incidents.

- **Regular Updates and Testing**: The disaster recovery plan should be regularly updated to reflect changes in the IT environment and business requirements. Regular testing of the plan is crucial to ensure its effectiveness and to make necessary adjustments.

Failover Mechanisms

- **Ensuring Business Continuity**: Implementing failover mechanisms for critical applications, especially those running on mainframes, is key to maintaining business operations during system outages.
- **Automatic Failover Systems**: These systems can automatically switch to a redundant or standby system in the event of a failure, minimizing service interruptions and downtime.
- **Load Balancing and Redundancy**: Techniques such as load balancing and maintaining redundant systems, both in the cloud and on-premises, help distribute the workload and reduce the risk of system overload, which can lead to failures.

Conclusion

In a hybrid environment, robust disaster recovery and data backup strategies are essential for safeguarding critical business data and ensuring continuous operation. Regular backups, combined with a well-planned and tested disaster recovery strategy and reliable failover mechanisms, provide a strong foundation for business resilience. These measures not only protect against data loss but also ensure that businesses can quickly recover and maintain operations in the face of unexpected disruptions.

Chapter 4: Networking and Connectivity in Hybrid Cloud Environments

In hybrid cloud environments, networking and connectivity are pivotal for integrating mainframe systems with cloud infrastructure. This chapter explores how to bridge the connectivity between these diverse systems, addressing both the challenges and solutions in managing a hybrid network.

Mainframe Connectivity: Legacy and Modern Protocols

- **Legacy Protocols**: Traditional mainframe systems often rely on legacy networking protocols that were standard when these systems were first developed. This includes protocols like SNA (Systems Network Architecture) and VTAM (Virtual Telecommunications Access Method).
- **Adapting to Modern Protocols**: For integration with cloud environments, mainframes often need to support modern networking protocols like TCP/IP. Adapting mainframe systems to work with these protocols is crucial for seamless connectivity with cloud-based systems.
- **Network Adapters and Gateways**: Using network adapters and gateways can facilitate the connectivity of

mainframes with modern network architectures, allowing legacy systems to communicate over contemporary network protocols.

Hybrid Cloud Networking: Bridging the Mainframe and Cloud Networks

- **Creating a Unified Network**: The goal of hybrid cloud networking is to create a unified network that seamlessly connects mainframe and cloud environments. This requires careful planning to ensure compatibility and optimal performance.
- **VPN and Direct Connect Solutions**: Solutions like Virtual Private Networks (VPNs) or dedicated direct connect services (such as AWS Direct Connect) can be used to establish secure, reliable connections between mainframe and cloud systems.
- **Network Virtualization**: Employing network virtualization can simplify network management and improve agility. It allows the creation of a logically abstracted network on top of the physical network infrastructure, making it easier to manage and configure the network to support diverse workloads.

Challenges and Solutions in Hybrid Network Management

- **Complexity in Integration**: One of the biggest challenges is the complexity of integrating disparate network systems and protocols. This can be addressed by using middleware and network integration tools that facilitate communication between different systems.
- **Ensuring Security and Compliance**: Maintaining security

and compliance across a hybrid network is critical. Implementing robust security measures like encryption, intrusion detection systems, and regular security audits can help mitigate risks.

- **Performance Optimization**: Ensuring optimal network performance in a hybrid environment involves regular monitoring and optimization. This includes managing bandwidth, latency, and ensuring the network is configured correctly for the specific needs of the workloads.
- **Scalability and Flexibility**: The network must be scalable and flexible to adapt to changing business needs. Cloud-based networking solutions can provide this scalability and flexibility, allowing for easy expansion or reconfiguration as required.

Conclusion

Networking and connectivity in hybrid cloud environments require a strategic approach to integrate mainframe systems with cloud infrastructure. By addressing the challenges in network management, employing modern connectivity solutions, and ensuring secure and efficient communication, organizations can effectively bridge the gap between mainframe and cloud environments. This integration is key to leveraging the combined strengths of both systems and achieving a cohesive and agile IT infrastructure.

4.1. Mainframe Connectivity: Legacy and Modern Protocols

The connectivity of mainframe systems in a hybrid cloud environment entails bridging the gap between legacy networking protocols inherent to mainframes and the modern protocols predominant in cloud computing. Let's explore these aspects in more detail:

Legacy Protocols

- **Systems Network Architecture (SNA)**: SNA is a proprietary IBM protocol suite developed in the 1970s for IBM mainframes. It was widely used for mainframe communication but is less compatible with the network architectures of today's cloud environments.
- **Virtual Telecommunications Access Method (VTAM)**: VTAM is another IBM mainframe protocol, primarily used for accessing data and managing network resources. Like SNA, VTAM is oriented towards traditional mainframe communication methods.

Adapting to Modern Protocols

- **Transition to TCP/IP**: The integration of mainframes with cloud environments necessitates the support of modern networking protocols, primarily TCP/IP (Transmission Control Protocol/Internet Protocol). TCP/IP is the backbone of the internet and modern network communications, offering a more universal and flexible approach to data transmission.

- **Protocol Conversion**: Adapting mainframe systems to work with TCP/IP often involves protocol conversion, where legacy data formats and protocols are translated into formats compatible with modern networking standards.
- **Software Upgrades**: In some cases, mainframe systems may require software upgrades to enable native support for TCP/IP, ensuring more efficient and direct communication with cloud-based systems.

Network Adapters and Gateways

- **Bridging the Gap**: Network adapters and gateways play a crucial role in facilitating the connectivity of mainframes to modern network architectures. They act as intermediaries that translate between the legacy protocols of the mainframe and the TCP/IP protocols used in cloud environments.
- **Hardware and Software Solutions**: This can involve both hardware solutions (like physical network adapters) and software solutions (such as gateways or middleware) that enable this translation and communication process.
- **Seamless Integration**: By employing these adapters and gateways, organizations can ensure that their legacy mainframe systems can communicate effectively over contemporary network protocols, thereby enabling seamless integration into a hybrid cloud environment.

Conclusion

The connectivity of mainframe systems in a hybrid cloud setup is a complex task that requires careful consideration of both legacy and modern networking protocols. By adapting mainframes to support TCP/IP, and using network adapters and gateways to facilitate communication, legacy mainframe systems can be effectively integrated into modern cloud-based network architectures. This integration is essential for organizations looking to leverage the power and reliability of mainframes while benefiting from the flexibility and scalability of cloud computing.

Legacy Protocols

Legacy networking protocols, such as IBM's Systems Network Architecture (SNA) and Virtual Telecommunications Access Method (VTAM), played a crucial role in the early days of mainframe communications. However, their compatibility with modern network architectures poses challenges in contemporary hybrid cloud environments. Let's delve deeper into these legacy protocols:

Systems Network Architecture (SNA)

- **Development and Purpose**: Developed by IBM in the 1970s, SNA was designed to provide a robust framework for mainframe communication, connecting various types of IBM computing devices and allowing them to communicate seamlessly.
- **Architecture and Components**: SNA is not a single protocol but a suite of structured protocols forming a complete architecture. It includes various components for data formatting, routing, and controlling communication among different nodes in a network.
- **Usage and Decline**: SNA was widely used in enterprise environments for mainframe communications, especially in large-scale IBM mainframe installations. However, its usage has declined with the advent of more open and flexible networking standards, particularly TCP/IP.

Virtual Telecommunications Access Method (VTAM)

- **Functionality**: VTAM, primarily used in IBM mainframe environments, is a control program for managing network resources and accessing data. It served as an integral part of SNA, handling communication tasks and providing an interface for network applications.

- **Role in Mainframe Communication**: VTAM played a key role in facilitating communication within SNA networks, managing sessions, and ensuring efficient data transfer between mainframe applications and network devices.
- **Transitioning from VTAM**: As network architectures evolved, the reliance on VTAM and its associated SNA framework has decreased. Modern mainframe environments often incorporate more contemporary networking protocols, moving away from the SNA and VTAM-centric models.

Conclusion

While SNA and VTAM were pioneering technologies in their time, shaping the way mainframes communicated, their compatibility with today's cloud-centric network architectures is limited. The transition from these legacy protocols to more universal standards like TCP/IP is a critical step in modernizing mainframe environments and integrating them into hybrid cloud infrastructures. This shift not only facilitates better communication and data transfer between disparate systems but also aligns mainframe networking with the broader, more interconnected IT landscape.

Adapting to Modern Protocols

Adapting mainframe systems to modern protocols, particularly TCP/IP, is a crucial step in facilitating their integration into hybrid cloud environments. This transition enables mainframes, traditionally operating on legacy protocols, to communicate effectively in the modern network landscape dominated by the internet and cloud services.

Transition to TCP/IP

- **Importance of TCP/IP**: The Transmission Control Protocol/Internet Protocol (TCP/IP) is the standard for data transmission over the internet and within most modern networked environments. It provides a universal set of rules for data transfer, ensuring interoperability between diverse systems and networks.
- **Benefits for Mainframes**: By supporting TCP/IP, mainframe systems gain enhanced capabilities to interact with a wide range of networks and services, particularly those in cloud environments. This support is vital for mainframes to remain relevant and functional in contemporary IT infrastructures.

Protocol Conversion

- **Bridging the Gap**: Transitioning from legacy protocols to TCP/IP typically involves protocol conversion. This process translates the data formats and communication protocols used in mainframes to those compatible with TCP/IP standards.
- **Integration Tools**: Various integration tools and middleware solutions are available to facilitate this conversion. They act as intermediaries, allowing

mainframes to communicate with TCP/IP networks without extensive modifications to the mainframe itself.

- **Maintaining Legacy Applications**: Protocol conversion allows existing legacy applications on mainframes to continue operating while enabling them to interact with newer network technologies. This is crucial for organizations looking to leverage their investment in mainframe applications while expanding their capabilities.

Software Upgrades

- **Updating Mainframe Software**: In some instances, mainframe systems may require software upgrades to enable native support for TCP/IP. This could include updating the operating system, networking software, or specific applications.
- **Enhancing Communication Efficiency**: Software upgrades can lead to more efficient and direct communication with cloud-based systems. By natively supporting TCP/IP, mainframes can reduce the need for complex conversions and intermediaries, leading to more streamlined and reliable data transfer.
- **Vendor Support**: Mainframe vendors often provide support and tools for these upgrades, ensuring that the transition to TCP/IP is as smooth as possible. They may offer specialized software packages or updates specifically designed to enhance TCP/IP compatibility and performance.

Conclusion

The adaptation of mainframe systems to modern networking protocols like TCP/IP is a critical process in the integration of these systems into hybrid cloud environments. Through protocol conversion and necessary software upgrades, mainframes can effectively communicate within the contemporary network landscape, ensuring their continued utility and efficiency in a cloud-dominated world. This transition not only extends the lifespan of mainframe investments but also opens up new possibilities for their use in modern computing scenarios.

Network Adapters and Gateways

Network adapters and gateways are essential components in modernizing the connectivity of mainframe systems, especially when integrating them into hybrid cloud environments. They serve as critical links that bridge the gap between the legacy communication protocols of mainframes and the modern TCP/IP protocols predominant in cloud networking.

Bridging the Gap

- **Intermediary Role**: Network adapters and gateways act as intermediaries or translators between the mainframe and cloud environments. They effectively translate the data and communication protocols from the mainframe's legacy systems to the TCP/IP protocols used in contemporary network architectures.
- **Facilitating Communication**: This role is crucial in enabling communication between systems that otherwise would not be able to interact due to incompatible protocols. Without these adapters and gateways, integrating mainframe systems with modern cloud infrastructure would be significantly more challenging.

Hardware and Software Solutions

- **Network Adapters**: On the hardware front, physical network adapters can be installed in mainframe systems. These adapters enable mainframes to connect to modern networks, converting legacy protocol communications into TCP/IP compatible signals.
- **Gateways and Middleware**: Software solutions, including gateways and middleware, provide a more flexible approach to protocol translation. These software solutions

can be configured to understand and translate a wide range of protocols, making them versatile tools in hybrid environments.

- **Customization and Configuration**: Both hardware and software solutions can often be customized and configured to meet the specific needs of an organization's network architecture, ensuring optimal compatibility and performance.

Seamless Integration

- **Enabling Effective Communication**: By using network adapters and gateways, organizations can ensure that their mainframe systems are not isolated from the rest of their IT infrastructure. This is particularly important for businesses that rely on the robust processing power of mainframes but also require the flexibility and scalability of cloud services.
- **Reducing Complexity**: These solutions simplify the complex process of integrating disparate networking systems. They allow organizations to maintain their existing mainframe investments while adopting new cloud technologies.
- **Supporting Hybrid Environments**: In hybrid cloud environments, seamless integration is key to achieving operational efficiency and agility. Network adapters and gateways play a pivotal role in making this possible, ensuring that data and resources can be shared and accessed across the hybrid landscape.

Conclusion

Network adapters and gateways are indispensable in the modernization of mainframe connectivity, particularly in the context of hybrid cloud integration. They provide the necessary bridge between legacy and modern networking protocols, enabling mainframe systems to effectively communicate within today's network architectures. This integration is fundamental for organizations looking to leverage the combined strengths of mainframe reliability and cloud computing's scalability and innovation.

4.2. Hybrid Cloud Networking: Bridging the Mainframe and Cloud Networks

Hybrid cloud networking plays a pivotal role in seamlessly integrating mainframe systems with cloud environments. The objective is to create a unified, efficient network infrastructure that supports the diverse needs of both mainframes and cloud-based resources. Let's explore the key strategies and technologies involved in this integration:

Creating a Unified Network

- **Seamless Connectivity**: The primary goal of hybrid cloud networking is to establish a network that facilitates seamless connectivity between mainframe and cloud environments. This unified network should enable smooth data flow and communication, ensuring that applications and services can operate efficiently across both platforms.
- **Compatibility and Performance**: Achieving this requires careful planning and execution, with a focus on ensuring compatibility between disparate network systems and optimizing performance. It involves understanding the unique networking requirements of both mainframes and cloud systems and designing a network that caters to these

needs.

VPN and Direct Connect Solutions

- **Virtual Private Networks (VPNs)**: VPNs create a secure, encrypted tunnel over the internet, allowing for safe communication between mainframe systems and cloud environments. This is particularly important for sensitive data transfers or for organizations with heightened security requirements.
- **Dedicated Direct Connect Services**: Services like AWS Direct Connect, Azure ExpressRoute, or Google Cloud Interconnect provide dedicated, private network connections between the mainframe and cloud infrastructures. These connections offer more reliable and consistent network performance compared to standard internet-based connections.
- **Security and Reliability**: Both VPNs and direct connect solutions enhance the security and reliability of network communications, which is crucial in a hybrid cloud setup where data often traverses public and private networks.

Network Virtualization

- **Abstracting the Physical Network**: Network virtualization involves creating a virtual, software-defined network that is abstracted from the physical network hardware. This virtual network can span across both mainframe and cloud environments, providing a flexible and manageable networking layer.
- **Agility and Simplified Management**: One of the key benefits of network virtualization is the agility it provides.

It allows IT teams to quickly configure and modify network settings without the need for physical changes to the network infrastructure. This is particularly useful in dynamic environments where workloads and resources may frequently change.

- **Support for Diverse Workloads**: Network virtualization facilitates the management and configuration of the network to support diverse workloads, ensuring that both mainframe and cloud applications have the network resources they require. It also enables better utilization of network resources and can improve overall network efficiency.

Conclusion

Bridging mainframe and cloud networks in a hybrid cloud setup involves a strategic combination of technologies like VPNs, direct connect services, and network virtualization. These technologies not only ensure secure and reliable connectivity but also provide the flexibility and agility needed to manage a diverse and dynamic network environment. The successful implementation of hybrid cloud networking is key to realizing the full potential of integrating mainframe robustness with cloud scalability and innovation.

Creating a Unified Network

Creating a unified network in a hybrid cloud environment is essential for achieving seamless connectivity between mainframe and cloud systems. This process requires a meticulous approach to ensure compatibility and optimal performance across diverse network architectures. Let's break down the key aspects of establishing such a network:

Seamless Connectivity

- **Integrating Diverse Environments**: The primary objective is to integrate the traditionally isolated mainframe environment with modern cloud infrastructures. This integration should facilitate uninterrupted data flow and communication, ensuring that applications and services can interact and function efficiently across both mainframe and cloud platforms.
- **Minimizing Latency and Maximizing Throughput**: Seamless connectivity involves not just the ability to communicate but to do so with minimal latency and maximum throughput. This is crucial for applications that rely on real-time data exchange or high-volume data processing.

Compatibility and Performance

- **Understanding Specific Requirements**: Different network systems, especially when comparing mainframes with cloud environments, have unique requirements and characteristics. For example, mainframes often deal with high-volume transaction processing, while cloud environments are designed for scalability and flexibility.
- **Designing for Coexistence**: The network design should

accommodate these varying requirements, ensuring that it can handle the high-speed, high-volume demands of mainframe applications while also providing the scalable, elastic bandwidth needed for cloud applications.

- **Network Topology and Technologies**: Careful consideration of network topology and the selection of appropriate networking technologies is essential. This might include the use of advanced routing protocols, software-defined networking (SDN), or specific WAN (Wide Area Network) technologies that can bridge the gap between mainframe and cloud systems.
- **Testing and Validation**: Before full-scale implementation, it's important to thoroughly test and validate the network design to ensure that it meets the required performance criteria and can handle the expected traffic loads without bottlenecks.

Conclusion

The creation of a unified network in a hybrid cloud setup is a strategic endeavor that requires a deep understanding of both mainframe and cloud networking principles. By focusing on seamless connectivity and ensuring compatibility and performance, organizations can build a robust network foundation that supports the efficient operation of both mainframe and cloud-based applications. This unified network is key to leveraging the strengths of both environments, leading to enhanced efficiency, agility, and scalability in the organization's overall IT infrastructure.

VPN and Direct Connect Solutions

VPN (Virtual Private Network) solutions and dedicated direct connect services are pivotal in establishing secure and reliable connections in hybrid cloud environments, especially when integrating mainframe systems with cloud infrastructures. These technologies play a crucial role in ensuring that data transfer between different environments is both secure and efficient.

Virtual Private Networks (VPNs)

- **Secure Encrypted Tunnel**: VPNs create an encrypted tunnel over the internet, providing a secure channel for data transfer. This encryption is crucial for protecting sensitive information as it moves between mainframes and cloud environments, safeguarding it from potential interception or unauthorized access.
- **Remote Accessibility**: VPNs are particularly beneficial for enabling remote access to mainframe systems. They allow users and applications in the cloud environment to securely access mainframe resources as if they were on the same local network.
- **Flexibility and Cost-Effectiveness**: VPNs offer a flexible and cost-effective solution for secure connectivity, especially for organizations that might not have the resources for more extensive networking infrastructure changes.

Dedicated Direct Connect Services

- **Private Network Connections**: Services like AWS Direct Connect, Azure ExpressRoute, and Google Cloud Interconnect provide dedicated network connections between mainframe systems and cloud infrastructures.

These are private connections that do not traverse the public internet.

- **Enhanced Performance and Reliability**: By using these direct connect services, organizations can achieve more consistent and reliable network performance. This is particularly important for applications that require high bandwidth or have low latency requirements.
- **Bypassing Public Internet Issues**: Dedicated connections mitigate many issues associated with the public internet, such as variable latency and congestion, which can be critical for certain mainframe applications and cloud services.

Security and Reliability

- **Enhanced Security**: Both VPNs and direct connect services enhance the security posture of an organization's network communications. VPNs achieve this through encryption, while direct connect services do so by providing a private pathway for data transfer.
- **Dependable Connectivity**: Reliability is a major advantage of these solutions. They offer a more dependable connectivity option compared to standard internet-based connections, which can be subject to a variety of performance and security issues.
- **Compliance Considerations**: For organizations in regulated industries, such as finance or healthcare, using VPNs or direct connect services can help meet compliance requirements related to data security and privacy.

Conclusion

In hybrid cloud networking, the use of VPNs and dedicated direct connect services is instrumental in achieving secure, reliable, and efficient connectivity between mainframe and cloud systems. These solutions not only facilitate safe data transfer but also ensure that the network performance meets the needs of critical business applications, making them indispensable in a well-integrated hybrid cloud setup.

Network Virtualization

Network virtualization plays a transformative role in hybrid cloud environments, especially when integrating mainframe systems with cloud infrastructures. By abstracting the complexities of physical networking, it offers a more agile and manageable approach to network management. Let's explore the facets of network virtualization in this context:

Abstracting the Physical Network

- **Creation of a Virtual Layer**: Network virtualization involves the creation of a virtual, software-defined network (SDN) that sits atop the physical network hardware. This abstraction allows the virtual network to extend seamlessly across different environments, including both mainframes and cloud systems.
- **Flexibility in Network Design**: The virtual network can be designed and structured independently of the physical network layout, providing a high degree of flexibility in how network resources are allocated and managed.

Agility and Simplified Management

- **Rapid Configuration Changes**: One of the most significant advantages of network virtualization is the ability to quickly reconfigure network settings. Changes that would traditionally require physical alterations to the network can now be made through software configurations, drastically reducing the time and effort involved.
- **Adaptability to Changing Needs**: In dynamic IT environments where workloads and resource demands frequently change, the agility provided by network

virtualization is invaluable. It allows for rapid adaptation to new requirements without the need for extensive network reengineering.

Support for Diverse Workloads

- **Tailored Network Resources**: Network virtualization enables the efficient allocation of network resources to different applications and workloads. This ensures that both mainframe applications, which might require robust and consistent network performance, and cloud applications, which may need scalable and flexible network services, are adequately supported.
- **Improved Network Utilization**: By virtualizing the network, resources can be better utilized, reducing waste and improving overall network efficiency. This is particularly beneficial in hybrid environments where the network needs to support a wide range of traffic types and volumes.
- **Enhanced Performance and Efficiency**: The ability to fine-tune network settings at the virtual layer allows for optimized performance for various applications. Network virtualization can also contribute to improved network efficiency by reducing bottlenecks and balancing loads more effectively.

Conclusion

Network virtualization offers a powerful solution for managing the complexities of networking in hybrid cloud environments. By providing a flexible, agile, and resource-efficient approach to network management, it plays a crucial role in ensuring that both mainframe and cloud systems can coexist and operate effectively within a unified network infrastructure. This technology not only simplifies network management but also supports the diverse and dynamic needs of modern IT workloads.

4.3. Challenges and Solutions in Hybrid Network Management

Managing a hybrid network that integrates mainframe and cloud environments presents a unique set of challenges. These challenges stem from the need to integrate diverse systems, ensure security and compliance, optimize performance, and maintain scalability and flexibility. Let's explore these challenges and their potential solutions:

Complexity in Integration

- **Integrating Different Systems**: One of the primary challenges in hybrid network management is the complexity of integrating network systems and protocols that were originally designed to operate independently. Mainframe systems often use different networking standards compared to modern cloud environments.
- **Solutions with Middleware and Tools**: The use of middleware and network integration tools can effectively address this challenge. These tools act as a bridge, facilitating communication and data exchange between disparate systems. They can translate network protocols and data formats, making them understandable across different network environments.

Ensuring Security and Compliance

- **Security Risks in Hybrid Networks**: As data moves between mainframe and cloud environments, it faces various security risks, including unauthorized access and data breaches.
- **Robust Security Measures**: Implementing comprehensive security measures such as encryption (for data in transit and at rest), intrusion detection systems, and conducting regular security audits are essential. These measures help in identifying vulnerabilities and mitigating potential risks.
- **Compliance with Regulations**: Maintaining compliance with relevant regulations (like GDPR, HIPAA, etc.) is crucial. This involves adhering to industry standards and best practices in data protection and privacy.

Performance Optimization

- **Network Efficiency**: In a hybrid environment, optimizing network performance for diverse workloads is essential. This includes ensuring sufficient bandwidth and minimizing latency.
- **Regular Monitoring and Management**: Continuous monitoring of network performance helps in identifying bottlenecks and areas for improvement. Tools for network traffic analysis and management can assist in optimizing the flow of data, ensuring that the network is configured to meet the specific requirements of different workloads.

Scalability and Flexibility

- **Adapting to Business Changes**: The network

infrastructure must be scalable and flexible to accommodate evolving business needs and varying workloads.

- **Leveraging Cloud-Based Solutions**: Cloud-based networking solutions offer considerable scalability and flexibility. They allow organizations to quickly scale up or down their network resources based on demand, without the need for significant physical infrastructure changes.
- **Software-Defined Networking (SDN)**: SDN can provide the agility needed in a hybrid environment, allowing network administrators to manage network services through abstraction of lower-level functionality. This is particularly useful for quickly adjusting network configurations in response to changing requirements.

Conclusion

Effective management of hybrid networks requires a multifaceted approach that addresses the integration of different systems, ensures robust security and compliance, optimizes performance, and maintains scalability and flexibility. By leveraging middleware, implementing comprehensive security strategies, continuously monitoring and optimizing performance, and utilizing cloud-based and software-defined networking solutions, organizations can overcome the challenges posed by hybrid network environments. This ensures a cohesive, efficient, and secure network infrastructure that supports the diverse needs of both mainframe and cloud systems.

Complexity in Integration

The complexity of integrating different network systems and protocols in a hybrid network environment, especially when combining mainframe and cloud systems, poses significant challenges. This complexity arises from the fundamental differences in the design and operation of these systems. Let's delve into these challenges and the solutions that middleware and network integration tools offer:

Integrating Different Systems

- **Divergent Networking Standards**: Traditional mainframe systems were built on networking standards and protocols quite distinct from those used in contemporary cloud-based environments. For instance, mainframes might use legacy protocols for communication, which are not natively compatible with the TCP/IP protocols predominantly used in cloud networks.
- **Operational Independence**: These systems were originally designed to operate independently, without the need for interaction with external networks or systems. As a result, integrating them into a hybrid network that includes modern cloud infrastructure requires overcoming significant technical hurdles.

Solutions with Middleware and Network Integration Tools

- **Bridging Communication Gaps**: Middleware and network integration tools play a crucial role in bridging the communication gap between mainframe and cloud systems. These solutions can effectively translate and facilitate the exchange of data between systems using different network protocols.

- **Protocol Translation**: One of the primary functions of these tools is to translate network protocols and data formats from the mainframe environment into formats compatible with cloud systems, and vice versa. This ensures that data can be accurately and efficiently exchanged across the hybrid network.
- **Seamless Integration**: By employing middleware, organizations can achieve a seamless integration of their mainframe systems with cloud infrastructures. This integration is essential for enabling unified operations and data management across the hybrid environment.
- **Enhancing Interoperability**: These tools enhance the interoperability of disparate systems, allowing them to communicate and function as a cohesive unit. This is particularly important for organizations looking to leverage the combined strengths of both mainframe and cloud capabilities.

Conclusion

The complexity in integrating mainframe systems with modern cloud environments in a hybrid network setup presents a significant challenge, primarily due to the differing network protocols and operational designs. Middleware and network integration tools provide a viable solution to this challenge, acting as intermediaries that facilitate communication and data exchange between these systems. By implementing these solutions, organizations can overcome the inherent complexities and ensure a smooth, efficient, and integrated hybrid network operation.

Ensuring Security and Compliance

Ensuring security and compliance in hybrid networks, where data flows between mainframe and cloud environments, is a critical aspect of maintaining the integrity and trustworthiness of an organization's IT infrastructure. The hybrid nature of these networks introduces a range of security challenges and necessitates strict adherence to regulatory requirements. Let's explore the strategies to address these concerns:

Security Risks in Hybrid Networks

- **Diverse Threat Landscape**: The hybrid network environment, combining legacy mainframe systems with modern cloud platforms, faces a diverse set of security threats. These include risks like unauthorized access, data breaches, and cyber-attacks that can exploit the vulnerabilities inherent in integrating disparate systems.
- **Data Movement Vulnerabilities**: As data moves between different environments (mainframe to cloud or vice versa), it becomes susceptible to interception, making secure data transfer mechanisms imperative.

Robust Security Measures

- **Encryption**: Implementing encryption for data at rest (stored data) and in transit (data being transferred) is fundamental in protecting sensitive information. Encryption acts as a critical barrier, preventing unauthorized access and ensuring data confidentiality.
- **Intrusion Detection Systems (IDS)**: Deploying IDS helps in continuously monitoring network traffic for suspicious activities and potential threats, thereby enabling timely detection and response to security incidents.

- **Regular Security Audits**: Conducting regular security audits is essential to identify and rectify vulnerabilities within the network. These audits can assess both technical and procedural aspects of the network's security posture.
- **Unified Security Policies**: In a hybrid environment, it's crucial to have unified security policies that encompass both mainframe and cloud components. This ensures consistent security management across the entire network.

Compliance with Regulations

- **Adhering to Regulatory Standards**: Compliance with data protection and privacy regulations such as the General Data Protection Regulation (GDPR), Health Insurance Portability and Accountability Act (HIPAA), and others is non-negotiable. These regulations set standards for handling sensitive data and impose penalties for non-compliance.
- **Data Governance Policies**: Establishing robust data governance policies helps in managing data in compliance with these regulations. This includes data classification, access controls, and regular reviews of data handling practices.
- **Continuous Compliance Monitoring**: Implementing tools and procedures for continuous compliance monitoring ensures that the network remains compliant with evolving regulations and standards.

Conclusion

In the context of hybrid networks, ensuring security and compliance is a multifaceted endeavor involving robust security measures like encryption and intrusion detection, regular audits, and strict adherence to regulatory standards. This comprehensive approach is essential not only for protecting sensitive data but also for maintaining the operational integrity of the network and upholding the organization's reputation and legal responsibilities. Effective management of these aspects is crucial in creating a secure and compliant hybrid network environment.

Performance Optimization

Optimizing network performance in a hybrid environment, which combines mainframe and cloud systems, is crucial for ensuring efficient operation across diverse workloads. Effective performance optimization involves a blend of ensuring network efficiency, regular monitoring, and proactive management. Let's delve into these aspects:

Network Efficiency

- **Ensuring Adequate Bandwidth**: Adequate bandwidth is essential to handle the data volume moving between mainframe and cloud environments. Insufficient bandwidth can lead to network congestion, negatively impacting the performance of applications and services.
- **Minimizing Latency**: Minimizing latency is particularly important for time-sensitive applications and can significantly affect user experience and application performance. Techniques like optimizing routing paths and using content delivery networks (CDNs) can help reduce latency.
- **Quality of Service (QoS) Settings**: Implementing QoS settings can prioritize critical network traffic, ensuring that high-priority data and applications receive the bandwidth they need, especially during peak usage times.

Regular Monitoring and Management

- **Continuous Performance Monitoring**: Regular monitoring of network performance is vital to identify potential issues like bottlenecks, which can impede data flow and degrade overall network efficiency.
- **Network Traffic Analysis**: Using network traffic analysis

tools can provide insights into how data travels through the network and how network resources are utilized. This information is critical for identifying inefficiencies and areas for optimization.

- **Proactive Network Management**: Proactive network management involves adjusting network configurations in response to changing conditions and demands. This might include rerouting traffic, scaling bandwidth up or down, or modifying load balancing strategies.
- **Predictive Analytics**: Advanced monitoring solutions can use predictive analytics to foresee potential network issues and allow IT teams to take preemptive action to mitigate them. This can be particularly beneficial in hybrid environments where network traffic patterns can be complex and dynamic.

Conclusion

Performance optimization in hybrid networks is a dynamic and ongoing process. It requires a balance between ensuring network efficiency through adequate bandwidth and minimized latency, and proactive network monitoring and management to adapt to changing demands and workloads. By regularly assessing network performance and utilizing advanced tools for traffic analysis and management, organizations can maintain an optimally performing hybrid network that supports the diverse needs of both mainframe and cloud-based applications.

Scalability and Flexibility

Scalability and flexibility are key components in managing hybrid networks, particularly in environments that integrate mainframes with cloud systems. As business needs and workloads evolve, the network infrastructure must be capable of adapting quickly and efficiently. This adaptability is crucial for maintaining operational efficiency and ensuring that the network can support varying demands. Let's explore how scalability and flexibility can be achieved in hybrid networks:

Adapting to Business Changes

- **Responsive to Evolving Needs**: A scalable and flexible network is essential for businesses to respond effectively to changing demands. This could involve handling increased data traffic, supporting new applications, or expanding into new geographic locations.
- **Modular Network Design**: Implementing a modular network design can facilitate scalability, allowing for easier expansion or modification of the network as business needs change.

Leveraging Cloud-Based Solutions

- **Dynamic Resource Allocation**: Cloud-based networking solutions are inherently scalable, offering the ability to dynamically allocate and adjust network resources based on current demands. This elasticity is a significant advantage, particularly for businesses experiencing fluctuating or unpredictable traffic patterns.
- **Cost-Effectiveness**: With cloud-based solutions, organizations can scale their network resources up or down as needed, often paying only for the resources they use.

This can lead to cost savings compared to maintaining a static, over-provisioned network infrastructure.

Software-Defined Networking (SDN)

- **Agile Network Management**: Software-Defined Networking (SDN) revolutionizes network management by separating the control plane (network intelligence and policy making) from the data plane (traffic forwarding). This abstraction allows for more agile and flexible network management.
- **Rapid Configuration Changes**: With SDN, network administrators can quickly adjust network configurations, set up new network segments, or apply new policies across the network through software interfaces, without the need to manually reconfigure individual network devices.
- **Enhanced Automation**: SDN enables enhanced automation capabilities in network management, allowing for more efficient use of network resources and quicker response to changing network conditions.

Conclusion

In a hybrid network environment, scalability and flexibility are vital in ensuring that the network can effectively support a range of business requirements and workloads. By leveraging cloud-based solutions and adopting technologies like Software-Defined Networking, organizations can create a network infrastructure that is not only robust and reliable but also agile and responsive to the dynamic needs of modern business operations. This adaptability is crucial for staying competitive in an increasingly digital and interconnected business landscape.

Chapter 5: Security and Compliance in Mainframe-Hybrid Cloud Ecosystems

In the intricate landscape of mainframe-hybrid cloud ecosystems, ensuring robust security and compliance is paramount. This chapter delves into the principles, regulatory requirements, and strategies essential for maintaining a secure and compliant hybrid environment.

Security Principles for Mainframes and Cloud Systems

- **Layered Security Approach**: Both mainframe and cloud systems should adopt a layered security approach. This includes perimeter defenses, internal network segmentation, access controls, and data encryption, both at rest and in transit.
- **Consistent Security Policies**: Establish unified security policies across both mainframe and cloud environments. Consistency in policies helps in managing security effectively, irrespective of where the data resides or is processed.
- **Regular Vulnerability Assessments**: Conducting regular security assessments, including penetration testing and

vulnerability scanning, ensures that potential security gaps are identified and addressed promptly.

Regulatory Compliance in Hybrid Cloud Operations

- **Understanding Specific Regulations**: Different industries are governed by various regulations that dictate how data should be managed and protected (e.g., GDPR for data privacy, HIPAA for healthcare, or PCI DSS for payment processing).
- **Data Sovereignty and Localization Laws**: Be aware of data sovereignty and localization laws, especially when dealing with cloud environments where data may be stored in multiple geographic locations.
- **Compliance Audits and Reporting**: Regular compliance audits are essential to verify that the hybrid environment adheres to the relevant legal and regulatory standards. Proper documentation and reporting mechanisms should be in place to demonstrate compliance.

Implementing Robust Security Measures in a Hybrid Setup

- **Data Encryption**: Implement strong encryption protocols for data at rest and in transit across both mainframe and cloud systems. Encryption is key to protecting sensitive data from unauthorized access.
- **Advanced Threat Detection and Response**: Utilize advanced threat detection systems, such as SIEM (Security Information and Event Management) and AI-driven threat analytics, to monitor and respond to security incidents promptly.
- **Access Control and Identity Management**: Implement

stringent access control measures. Use identity and access management (IAM) solutions to ensure that only authorized personnel have access to sensitive systems and data.

- **Secure API Gateways**: When integrating mainframe and cloud systems, secure API gateways are crucial for protecting the data exchange and ensuring that only authorized applications and services can communicate with each other.
- **Employee Training and Awareness**: Regular training programs for employees to raise awareness about cybersecurity risks and best practices are essential. Human error often poses a significant risk to system security.

Conclusion

Security and compliance in mainframe-hybrid cloud ecosystems require a comprehensive and proactive approach. By integrating robust security measures, adhering to regulatory compliance, and continuously monitoring and adjusting strategies in response to evolving threats and regulations, organizations can ensure a secure and compliant hybrid environment. This is crucial not only for protecting sensitive data but also for maintaining trust and meeting the legal obligations inherent in modern business operations.

5.1. Security Principles for Mainframes and Cloud Systems

In the realm of mainframe-hybrid cloud ecosystems, adhering to robust security principles is essential to safeguard sensitive data and maintain system integrity. The combination of mainframes and cloud systems presents unique security challenges that require a multifaceted approach. Let's explore these security principles in detail:

Layered Security Approach

- **Perimeter Defenses**: This involves protecting the network boundaries using firewalls, intrusion prevention systems (IPS), and similar tools. Perimeter defenses are the first line of defense against external threats.
- **Internal Network Segmentation**: Segmenting the network internally can help contain breaches and limit the spread of attacks within the system. This can be particularly effective in minimizing the impact of a breach in a hybrid environment.
- **Access Controls**: Implement robust access control mechanisms to ensure only authorized personnel have access to sensitive systems and data. This includes role-based access control (RBAC) and the principle of least

privilege.

- **Data Encryption**: Encrypting data both at rest (when stored) and in transit (during transfer) is crucial to protect sensitive information from unauthorized access and breaches. This is particularly important in hybrid environments where data frequently moves between different systems and networks.

Consistent Security Policies

- **Unified Policies Across Environments**: Establishing consistent security policies across mainframe and cloud environments ensures that security is uniformly managed and enforced, regardless of where data resides or is processed.
- **Policy Management and Review**: Regularly review and update security policies to reflect new threats, technological changes, and compliance requirements. This includes policies for data handling, user authentication, and incident response.

Regular Vulnerability Assessments

- **Proactive Security Checks**: Regularly conducting security assessments such as penetration testing and vulnerability scanning is vital in identifying and addressing potential security vulnerabilities before they can be exploited.
- **Continuous Monitoring**: Implement continuous monitoring strategies to detect anomalies, suspicious activities, or unauthorized access attempts in real-time. This can be facilitated by advanced monitoring tools and security information and event management (SIEM)

systems.

- **Response and Remediation Plans**: In conjunction with assessments, develop and maintain incident response and remediation plans to quickly address any identified security issues. This includes having a clear protocol for patch management and system updates.

Conclusion

Adhering to these security principles is key to protecting mainframe-hybrid cloud ecosystems. A layered security approach, consistent security policies, and regular vulnerability assessments form a comprehensive defense strategy against a wide range of security threats. By implementing these measures, organizations can enhance the security posture of their hybrid environments, ensuring the protection and integrity of their critical systems and data.

Layered Security Approach

The layered security approach is a comprehensive strategy for safeguarding mainframe-hybrid cloud ecosystems. By implementing multiple layers of defense, organizations can protect against a wide range of security threats, both external and internal. Let's delve deeper into each layer of this approach:

Perimeter Defenses

- **Firewalls**: Firewalls act as a barrier between trusted internal networks and untrusted external networks, such as the internet. They control incoming and outgoing network traffic based on predetermined security rules.
- **Intrusion Prevention Systems (IPS)**: IPS monitors network traffic to detect and prevent attempted cyberattacks. By analyzing traffic patterns, IPS can identify and block malicious activities and known threats.
- **Additional Perimeter Tools**: Other perimeter defense tools can include VPN gateways for secure remote access, email security gateways to filter malicious emails, and Web Application Firewalls (WAFs) to protect web applications from attacks.

Internal Network Segmentation

- **Dividing the Network**: Segmenting the network into smaller, controlled segments or subnets helps in containing potential breaches. This means that if a breach occurs in one segment, it does not automatically compromise the entire network.
- **Use of VLANs and SDN**: Technologies like Virtual Local Area Networks (VLANs) and Software-Defined Networking (SDN) can facilitate network segmentation.

They allow network administrators to logically divide the network and control traffic flow between segments.

Access Controls

- **Role-Based Access Control (RBAC)**: RBAC ensures that access to resources is granted based on the roles of individual users within the organization. Users are granted permission to access only what they need to perform their job functions.
- **Least Privilege Principle**: Implementing the principle of least privilege means users are given the minimum level of access required to perform their duties. This reduces the risk of unauthorized access to sensitive systems and data.
- **Multi-Factor Authentication (MFA)**: MFA adds an extra layer of security by requiring users to provide two or more verification factors to gain access to resources.

Data Encryption

- **Encrypting Data at Rest**: Protecting stored data with encryption safeguards it from unauthorized access and breaches. This is critical for sensitive data stored in databases, file systems, and cloud storage.
- **Encrypting Data in Transit**: As data moves across networks, including between mainframes and cloud environments, it should be encrypted to prevent interception and unauthorized access. Secure protocols like TLS (Transport Layer Security) should be used for transmitting data.

Conclusion

A layered security approach is essential in protecting mainframe-hybrid cloud ecosystems. By combining perimeter defenses, internal network segmentation, stringent access controls, and data encryption, organizations can create a robust security posture that defends against diverse threats. This comprehensive strategy is crucial in safeguarding sensitive data and maintaining the integrity of the network infrastructure.

Consistent Security Policies

The implementation of consistent security policies across mainframe and cloud environments is a critical element in the overarching security strategy of a hybrid IT infrastructure. Uniform policies help in creating a cohesive security posture that effectively addresses the unique challenges of a hybrid environment. Let's explore these aspects in more detail:

Unified Policies Across Environments

- **Harmonization of Security Measures**: Developing security policies that are uniformly applicable across both mainframe and cloud environments helps in harmonizing security measures. This uniformity is crucial to avoid gaps in security that can arise due to disparate policy frameworks.
- **Seamless Security Management**: Consistent policies ensure that security is managed and enforced cohesively, irrespective of whether the data is stored on a mainframe or in the cloud, or whether it's being processed or in transit. This holistic approach is key to protecting the integrity and confidentiality of data across the entire IT landscape.

Policy Management and Review

- **Regular Policy Updates**: The cybersecurity landscape is continuously evolving, with new threats emerging regularly. Regularly reviewing and updating security policies ensures that they remain effective against current threats and vulnerabilities.
- **Reflecting Technological and Regulatory Changes**: Security policies should be updated to reflect not only new

threats but also changes in technology and regulatory requirements. For instance, the adoption of new cloud technologies or changes in data protection regulations like GDPR or HIPAA should be reflected in the security policies.

- **Comprehensive Policy Framework**: The security policy framework should cover all critical aspects of cybersecurity, including data handling and classification, user authentication protocols, network access controls, incident response mechanisms, and data breach notification procedures.
- **Employee Training and Awareness**: Part of effective policy management is ensuring that all employees are aware of and understand the security policies. Regular training sessions and updates can help inculcate a culture of security awareness throughout the organization.

Conclusion

Consistent security policies are the backbone of a robust security strategy in a mainframe-hybrid cloud ecosystem. By establishing unified policies and regularly updating them to reflect the dynamic nature of cyber threats, technological advancements, and compliance mandates, organizations can ensure a strong and cohesive defense against potential security breaches. This approach not only safeguards critical data and systems but also reinforces the organization's commitment to security and compliance.

Regular Vulnerability Assessments

Regular vulnerability assessments are an essential component of a proactive security strategy, especially in complex mainframe-hybrid cloud environments. These assessments help in identifying and mitigating potential vulnerabilities before they can be exploited by malicious actors. Let's delve into the key aspects of regular vulnerability assessments:

Proactive Security Checks

- **Penetration Testing**: Penetration testing involves simulating cyberattacks to assess the security of the system. It helps in identifying vulnerabilities that could be exploited by attackers, providing valuable insights into the effectiveness of existing security measures.
- **Vulnerability Scanning**: Regular vulnerability scanning is crucial for detecting potential security weaknesses in the network, software, and systems. Automated scanning tools can frequently assess the infrastructure for known vulnerabilities, ensuring timely identification of risks.
- **Comprehensive Assessment**: It's important that these assessments cover all aspects of the hybrid environment, including mainframe-specific vulnerabilities, cloud services, and the interfaces between them.

Continuous Monitoring

- **Real-time Anomaly Detection**: Continuous monitoring of the network and systems enables the detection of anomalies, suspicious activities, and potential unauthorized access attempts as they occur. This real-time surveillance is vital for promptly identifying and responding to potential security incidents.

- **Utilizing SIEM Systems**: Security Information and Event Management (SIEM) systems can aggregate and analyze data from various sources to provide a comprehensive view of the security status. SIEM systems can help in detecting patterns and trends that might indicate a security threat.

Response and Remediation Plans

- **Incident Response Protocols**: Alongside regular assessments, having well-defined incident response and remediation plans is critical. These plans should outline clear procedures for responding to detected security incidents, ensuring a quick and coordinated reaction to mitigate the impact.
- **Patch Management**: Regular updates and patch management are key components of remediation. Keeping software and systems up-to-date with the latest patches is crucial in protecting against known vulnerabilities.
- **Continuous Improvement**: Incident response plans should be regularly reviewed and updated based on the findings from vulnerability assessments and real-world incidents. This helps in continuously improving the security posture and response capabilities.

Conclusion

Regular vulnerability assessments, coupled with continuous monitoring and robust incident response plans, form the cornerstone of a proactive security approach in mainframe-hybrid cloud environments. By regularly evaluating the security of the system and being prepared to respond effectively to any incidents, organizations can significantly enhance their defense against cyber threats and maintain a secure and resilient IT infrastructure.

5.2. Regulatory Compliance in Hybrid Cloud Operations

Regulatory compliance is a critical aspect of managing hybrid cloud operations, particularly when these operations span various jurisdictions and involve handling sensitive data. Different industries are subject to specific regulations, and adherence to these is mandatory to avoid legal repercussions and maintain trust. Here's a deeper look into the key areas of regulatory compliance in hybrid cloud operations:

Understanding Specific Regulations

- **Industry-Specific Regulations**: Different industries are subject to specific regulations designed to protect sensitive data. For instance, the General Data Protection Regulation (GDPR) governs data privacy in the European Union, the Health Insurance Portability and Accountability Act (HIPAA) sets standards for patient data privacy in healthcare in the United States, and the Payment Card Industry Data Security Standard (PCI DSS) regulates how payment card information should be handled.
- **Customized Compliance Strategies**: Compliance strategies should be tailored to these specific regulations, taking into account the type of data handled, the nature of

the business, and the jurisdictions in which the company operates.

Data Sovereignty and Localization Laws

- **Understanding Data Residency Requirements**: Data sovereignty and localization laws dictate where and how data should be stored and processed. This is especially important in cloud environments, where data might be stored in data centers located in different countries.
- **Navigating Multi-Jurisdictional Challenges**: For organizations operating internationally, it's essential to understand and comply with the data residency and sovereignty laws of all the jurisdictions they operate in. This may require storing and processing data locally in each jurisdiction or adhering to cross-border data transfer rules.

Compliance Audits and Reporting

- **Regular Compliance Audits**: Conducting regular audits is vital to ensure that the hybrid cloud environment remains compliant with all relevant regulations and standards. Audits can identify areas where the organization might be at risk of non-compliance.
- **Documentation and Reporting**: Maintaining thorough documentation of compliance efforts and having robust reporting mechanisms in place are crucial. This not only aids in audits but also serves as proof of compliance in case of regulatory inquiries or investigations.
- **Continuous Compliance Monitoring**: Implementing continuous monitoring tools can help in keeping track of compliance in real-time, alerting to potential compliance

issues as they arise.

Conclusion

Regulatory compliance in hybrid cloud operations is a complex but essential component of data management and security. By understanding specific regulations, adhering to data sovereignty and localization laws, and conducting regular audits and reporting, organizations can ensure that they operate legally and ethically in their handling of sensitive data. This adherence not only protects the organization from legal risks but also builds trust with customers and stakeholders.

Understanding Specific Regulations

Understanding specific regulations and tailoring compliance strategies accordingly is crucial for organizations operating within mainframe-hybrid cloud ecosystems. Each industry faces unique regulatory demands, particularly concerning data privacy and security. Let's delve into how organizations can navigate these regulatory landscapes:

Industry-Specific Regulations

- **GDPR (General Data Protection Regulation)**: GDPR imposes strict rules on data privacy and the handling of personal data for entities operating in the European Union. It emphasizes user consent, data minimization, and the right to data access and erasure.
- **HIPAA (Health Insurance Portability and Accountability Act)**: In the U.S., HIPAA regulates the use and disclosure of Protected Health Information (PHI) in the healthcare sector. It requires safeguards to ensure the confidentiality, integrity, and security of PHI.
- **PCI DSS (Payment Card Industry Data Security Standard)**: PCI DSS sets the operational and technical standards for organizations handling credit and debit card transactions. It mandates measures to protect cardholder data against unauthorized access.

Customized Compliance Strategies

- **Tailoring Strategies to Specific Needs**: Compliance strategies should be customized based on the type of data handled, the specific regulatory requirements of the industry, and the geographical location of the company and its customers.

- **Data Classification and Handling**: Classifying data based on sensitivity and regulatory requirements is essential. For example, PHI data in healthcare must be treated differently from financial data in banking sectors.
- **Jurisdictional Awareness**: For organizations operating in multiple jurisdictions, understanding and complying with the laws of each region is vital. This includes adhering to cross-border data transfer rules and regional privacy laws.
- **Incorporating Best Practices**: Beyond meeting regulatory requirements, incorporating industry best practices and standards (such as ISO 27001 for information security management) can further strengthen compliance strategies.

Conclusion

Navigating the regulatory landscape in mainframe-hybrid cloud ecosystems requires a deep understanding of specific industry regulations and the development of tailored compliance strategies. By focusing on these aspects, organizations can not only ensure compliance with various data protection and privacy laws but also foster trust with clients and stakeholders, maintaining a reputation for responsible data management and security.

Data Sovereignty and Localization Laws

Data sovereignty and localization laws are crucial considerations in the management of hybrid cloud environments, particularly for organizations that operate across multiple jurisdictions. These laws can significantly impact how and where data is stored and processed. Let's explore these aspects in more detail:

Understanding Data Residency Requirements

- **Local Storage and Processing**: Data sovereignty laws require that data is stored and processed within the geographical boundaries of a specific country or region. This is particularly pertinent in cloud environments, where data centers are often spread across various global locations.
- **Implications for Cloud Storage**: Organizations must ensure that their cloud storage and processing strategies comply with these laws, which may involve using data centers located in specific countries or regions to store and process data.

Navigating Multi-Jurisdictional Challenges

- **Compliance in Multiple Regions**: For international organizations, compliance with data sovereignty and localization laws can be complex, as they need to navigate the laws of each country or region they operate in.
- **Local Storage Solutions**: In some cases, this may mean setting up localized data storage solutions in each jurisdiction to ensure compliance. Cloud service providers often offer region-specific storage options to assist with this.
- **Cross-Border Data Transfer Regulations**: In addition to local storage requirements, organizations must also be

aware of and comply with regulations governing the transfer of data across borders. This includes understanding and adhering to international agreements and frameworks such as the EU-U.S. Privacy Shield or standard contractual clauses for data transfer.

- **Legal and Technical Expertise**: Navigating these multi-jurisdictional challenges often requires both legal and technical expertise to ensure that data handling practices are compliant in all operating regions. It may involve close collaboration between legal teams, IT departments, and cloud service providers.

Conclusion

Data sovereignty and localization laws present significant challenges for organizations operating in hybrid cloud environments, especially those spanning multiple jurisdictions. Understanding and adhering to these laws is crucial to ensure legal compliance and to maintain the trust of customers and stakeholders. It requires a careful and well-informed approach to data storage and processing, as well as a thorough understanding of the complexities involved in cross-border data transfer.

Compliance Audits and Reporting

Compliance audits and reporting are essential components in the governance of mainframe-hybrid cloud environments, especially given the complex regulatory landscape that organizations must navigate. Regular audits, comprehensive documentation, and continuous monitoring are key practices that ensure ongoing compliance. Let's explore these in more detail:

Regular Compliance Audits

- **Identifying Compliance Risks**: Regular audits are critical for assessing whether the hybrid cloud environment adheres to applicable laws and regulations. They help identify areas of potential non-compliance and vulnerabilities that could lead to legal or regulatory issues.
- **Audit Scope and Frequency**: The scope and frequency of these audits should be determined based on factors such as the organization's size, complexity of the hybrid environment, and the regulatory landscape. More frequent audits may be necessary in highly regulated industries or in environments with rapidly changing technologies and processes.
- **Engaging External Auditors**: In some cases, it may be beneficial to engage external auditors who specialize in specific regulations or technologies to gain an objective assessment of compliance status.

Documentation and Reporting

- **Maintaining Compliance Records**: Keeping detailed records of compliance efforts is crucial. This includes documentation of policies and procedures, audit reports, training records, and any corrective actions taken in response to audit findings.

- **Evidence of Compliance**: These documents serve as evidence of compliance efforts and are invaluable in the event of regulatory inquiries or investigations. They demonstrate the organization's commitment to adhering to regulatory standards and can be pivotal in mitigating legal risks.
- **Reporting Mechanisms**: Establish robust mechanisms for reporting compliance status to stakeholders, including management, regulatory bodies, and customers. Transparency in reporting can build trust and demonstrate the organization's commitment to regulatory compliance.

Continuous Compliance Monitoring

- **Real-Time Compliance Tracking**: Implementing tools for continuous monitoring of compliance helps in maintaining a real-time overview of the organization's adherence to relevant regulations. This proactive approach enables quick identification and remediation of potential compliance issues.
- **Automated Alerts and Notifications**: Advanced monitoring tools can provide automated alerts when potential non-compliance issues are detected, allowing for immediate action to rectify the situation.
- **Integration with IT Systems**: Ensure that continuous monitoring tools are well-integrated with the IT infrastructure, including both mainframe and cloud components, for comprehensive coverage.

Conclusion

In a mainframe-hybrid cloud environment, conducting regular compliance audits, maintaining rigorous documentation and reporting, and implementing continuous compliance monitoring are fundamental practices. These efforts not only ensure adherence to legal and regulatory requirements but also bolster the organization's position in the event of external audits or investigations. Effective compliance management is a dynamic process that requires ongoing attention and adaptation to changes in both the regulatory landscape and the technology environment.

5.3. Implementing Robust Security Measures in a Hybrid Setup

Implementing robust security measures is critical in a hybrid setup that integrates mainframes with cloud systems. This integration often creates a complex security landscape that requires advanced strategies to protect sensitive data and maintain system integrity. Let's delve into key strategies for enhancing security in a hybrid environment:

Data Encryption

- **Encrypting Sensitive Data**: Strong encryption protocols for data at rest (stored data) and in transit (data being moved) are essential. Encryption serves as a fundamental barrier, securing sensitive data against unauthorized access, interception, and theft.
- **Encryption Across Environments**: Ensuring that encryption is consistently applied across both mainframe and cloud environments is crucial. This includes encrypting database files, backups, and data transfers between different systems.

Advanced Threat Detection and Response

- **SIEM Systems**: Security Information and Event Management (SIEM) systems provide real-time analysis of security alerts generated by applications and network hardware. They help in detecting, analyzing, and responding to security incidents.
- **AI-Driven Threat Analytics**: Leveraging artificial intelligence for threat detection and response can enhance the ability to identify and react to sophisticated cyber threats. AI-driven systems can analyze patterns and predict potential security breaches more efficiently.

Access Control and Identity Management

- **Implementing IAM Solutions**: Identity and Access Management (IAM) solutions are key to managing user identities and controlling access to resources within the hybrid environment. This includes managing user credentials, enforcing access policies, and monitoring user activities.
- **Role-Based Access Controls (RBAC)**: RBAC ensures that access to systems and data is based on the user's role within the organization, providing access only to what is necessary for their job functions.

Secure API Gateways

- **Safeguarding Data Exchange**: Secure API gateways are critical when integrating mainframe and cloud systems. They manage and secure the APIs that facilitate communication and data exchange between different systems.
- **Controlling Access**: These gateways can control access to

APIs, ensuring that only authorized applications and services can interact, thus preventing unauthorized data access or manipulation.

Employee Training and Awareness

- **Cybersecurity Training Programs**: Regular training and awareness programs for employees are crucial in mitigating the risk of human error, which is a significant factor in many security breaches.
- **Building a Security Culture**: Educating staff about cybersecurity risks, best practices, and procedures helps in fostering a culture of security within the organization. This includes training on recognizing phishing attempts, proper handling of sensitive data, and reporting suspicious activities.

Conclusion

In a hybrid environment, robust security measures are vital to protect against the diverse range of threats that both mainframe and cloud systems face. Implementing strong encryption, advanced threat detection systems, stringent access control, secure API gateways, and comprehensive employee training and awareness programs are key strategies to enhance security. These measures collectively form a comprehensive defense, safeguarding sensitive data and systems while ensuring the integrity and reliability of the hybrid IT infrastructure.

Data Encryption

Data encryption is a cornerstone in the security framework of any hybrid cloud-mainframe ecosystem. It plays a pivotal role in safeguarding sensitive data against a range of cyber threats, including unauthorized access, interception, and theft. Let's delve into the specifics of implementing data encryption in such an environment:

Encrypting Sensitive Data

- **Data at Rest**: Encrypting data at rest involves securing stored data on physical media, whether it's on mainframe systems or cloud storage. This is crucial for protecting sensitive information like personal data, financial records, or intellectual property from being accessed if the storage medium is compromised.
- **Data in Transit**: Encryption of data in transit is equally important. As data moves between mainframes, cloud services, and end-users, it is vulnerable to interception. Encrypting this data ensures that even if it is intercepted, it remains unreadable and secure.

Encryption Across Environments

- **Consistent Application**: It's vital to ensure that encryption protocols are consistently applied across both mainframe and cloud environments. Inconsistencies in encryption can create vulnerabilities that can be exploited by cyber attackers.
- **Database and File Encryption**: This includes implementing encryption for database files, which often house sensitive data. Encrypting backups is also essential to protect data during storage and transfer to off-site locations.

- **Secure Data Transfer Protocols**: When transferring data between systems, secure transfer protocols such as SFTP (Secure File Transfer Protocol) or HTTPS (Hypertext Transfer Protocol Secure) should be used. These protocols provide an additional layer of security by encrypting the data during transmission.
- **Key Management**: Effective key management is an integral part of a robust encryption strategy. This includes securely storing encryption keys, regularly changing them, and ensuring they are accessible only to authorized entities.

Conclusion

In summary, implementing strong encryption protocols for data at rest and in transit, and ensuring consistent encryption across mainframe and cloud environments, are fundamental to protecting sensitive data in a hybrid ecosystem. This approach forms a crucial barrier against data breaches, ensuring the confidentiality and integrity of sensitive information across diverse and complex IT environments. Effective encryption, combined with proper key management, provides a strong foundation for a comprehensive data security strategy.

Advanced Threat Detection and Response

Advanced threat detection and response mechanisms are essential in safeguarding hybrid cloud-mainframe ecosystems from increasingly sophisticated cyber threats. These mechanisms, including SIEM systems and AI-driven threat analytics, play a crucial role in the proactive identification and mitigation of security risks. Let's delve deeper into these technologies:

SIEM Systems

- **Real-Time Security Monitoring**: Security Information and Event Management (SIEM) systems collect and aggregate log data generated by applications, network hardware, and security devices across the hybrid environment. This data includes everything from network traffic logs to user activities.
- **Incident Detection and Analysis**: SIEM systems analyze this data in real-time to identify abnormal patterns or indicators of potential security incidents. This can include detecting unusual access patterns that may indicate a breach, or identifying trends that could suggest a developing threat.
- **Facilitating Rapid Response**: Upon detecting a potential security issue, SIEM systems can alert security teams, providing them with detailed information to facilitate a rapid response. Some SIEM systems also offer automated response capabilities, which can initiate predefined actions to contain and mitigate threats.

AI-Driven Threat Analytics

- **Enhanced Detection Capabilities**: Integrating artificial intelligence (AI) into threat detection systems enhances the ability to identify complex and subtle cyber threats that traditional systems might miss. AI algorithms can process vast amounts of data and recognize patterns indicative of malicious activity.

- **Predictive Analytics**: AI-driven systems can go beyond detecting existing threats; they can also predict potential future security breaches based on evolving patterns and trends in the data. This predictive capability is particularly useful in identifying and thwarting advanced persistent threats (APTs) and zero-day attacks.
- **Automated Learning and Adaptation**: One of the key strengths of AI in cybersecurity is its ability to learn and adapt over time. As the system is exposed to more data, it becomes more accurate and efficient in detecting and responding to threats, continuously improving the organization's security posture.

Conclusion

In the complex landscape of mainframe-hybrid cloud environments, advanced threat detection and response systems, including SIEM and AI-driven threat analytics, are indispensable. They provide comprehensive monitoring, rapid detection, and effective response capabilities, which are crucial in identifying and mitigating sophisticated cyber threats. The integration of these advanced technologies into an organization's security strategy significantly strengthens its defense against a wide array of cyber risks, ensuring the resilience and integrity of its critical IT infrastructure.

Access Control and Identity Management

Access control and identity management are pivotal elements in securing a mainframe-hybrid cloud environment. Effective management of user access and identities is crucial to protect sensitive information and systems from unauthorized use. Implementing Identity and Access Management (IAM) solutions and Role-Based Access Control (RBAC) are essential strategies in this regard:

Implementing IAM Solutions

- **Managing User Identities**: IAM solutions are crucial for managing the identities of users across the hybrid environment. This includes the creation, maintenance, and deletion of user accounts, along with managing their credentials.
- **Enforcing Access Policies**: IAM systems enforce access policies that define who can access what resources and under what conditions. These policies are crucial for controlling access to sensitive data and critical systems.
- **Monitoring User Activities**: Continuous monitoring of user activities helps in detecting any unusual or unauthorized actions. IAM solutions can provide detailed logs and reports on user activities, which are valuable for both security and compliance purposes.
- **Integrating with Existing Systems**: For effective implementation, IAM solutions must be integrated with existing systems in both the mainframe and cloud environments. This ensures a unified approach to access management across all platforms.

Role-Based Access Controls (RBAC)

- **Access Based on Role**: RBAC is a method of restricting system access to authorized users based on their roles within the organization. Each role is assigned specific access rights, and users are granted permissions based on their assigned role.
- **Minimizing Privilege Access**: RBAC adheres to the principle of least privilege, ensuring users have access only to the resources necessary for their job functions. This reduces the risk of unauthorized access to sensitive data.
- **Simplifying Management**: Implementing RBAC simplifies the management of user permissions, as changes in roles can automatically adjust a user's access rights. This is particularly useful in large organizations or in environments with high employee turnover.
- **Dynamic Role Assignments**: In a hybrid environment, roles can be dynamically assigned and adjusted based on changing needs and conditions, providing flexibility and enhancing security.

Conclusion

In a mainframe-hybrid cloud environment, robust access control and identity management are essential for safeguarding sensitive data and systems. Implementing comprehensive IAM solutions and utilizing RBAC are effective strategies to manage access privileges, monitor user activities, and ensure that users have appropriate access as per their role in the organization. These measures not only enhance security but also play a significant role in maintaining regulatory compliance and operational efficiency.

Secure API Gateways

Secure API gateways play a crucial role in the security architecture of mainframe-hybrid cloud ecosystems. As intermediaries, they manage and secure the Application

Programming Interfaces (APIs) that facilitate communication and data exchange between disparate systems. Let's explore their significance in more detail:

Safeguarding Data Exchange

- **API Security**: In a hybrid environment where mainframes and cloud systems interact, APIs are often the glue that binds different platforms. Secure API gateways act as a protective layer for these APIs, ensuring that all data exchanges via APIs are secure and protected against threats like data breaches or API abuses.
- **Encryption and Protocol Management**: Secure gateways typically encrypt data transmitted through APIs and manage protocol translations, ensuring that communication between mainframe and cloud systems is both secure and efficient.

Controlling Access

- **Access Management**: Secure API gateways control who and what can communicate through the APIs. They can authenticate and authorize API requests, ensuring that only authorized applications, services, and users can access and interact with the APIs.
- **Rate Limiting and Traffic Control**: These gateways can also implement rate limiting and traffic control to prevent abuse and overloading of APIs. This is particularly important to protect against denial-of-service (DoS) attacks and other malicious activities aimed at disrupting the API services.
- **API Auditing and Logging**: Secure gateways often provide auditing and logging capabilities, enabling detailed

monitoring of API usage. This not only aids in security but also helps in compliance and troubleshooting.

Conclusion

In the integration of mainframe and cloud systems, secure API gateways are indispensable for ensuring that API-driven communications and data exchanges are protected. By managing access, encrypting data, and providing monitoring capabilities, these gateways form a critical component of the security infrastructure, safeguarding against unauthorized access and potential API-related vulnerabilities. Implementing secure API gateways is a key step in building a robust and secure mainframe-hybrid cloud environment.

Employee Training and Awareness

Employee training and awareness are vital components of a comprehensive cybersecurity strategy, especially in environments where mainframe systems are integrated with cloud technologies. Human error is often cited as one of the leading causes of security breaches, making regular training and the establishment of a security-conscious culture within the organization imperative. Let's explore these aspects in more detail:

Cybersecurity Training Programs

- **Regular and Updated Training**: Conducting regular cybersecurity training programs ensures that all employees, regardless of their role, are aware of the latest cyber threats and the best practices to mitigate them. Training should be updated frequently to reflect the evolving nature of cyber threats.
- **Practical and Engaging Content**: Training programs should be practical and engaging, with real-world scenarios and interactive elements to help employees understand the relevance of cybersecurity in their daily work.
- **Role-Specific Training**: Tailoring training programs to specific roles can be effective, especially for staff with access to sensitive systems or data. For example, IT personnel may require more in-depth technical training compared to other employees.

Building a Security Culture

- **Promoting Awareness**: Continuous efforts to promote cybersecurity awareness help in building a culture where security is a shared responsibility. This includes regular communication about potential threats and reminders of security protocols.

- **Recognizing and Reporting Threats**: Employees should be trained to recognize common threats such as phishing emails and social engineering attacks. They should also know the procedures for reporting any suspicious activities or potential security incidents.
- **Data Handling and Privacy**: Training should also cover the proper handling of sensitive data, understanding privacy regulations relevant to the organization's operations, and the importance of compliance.
- **Incentivizing Secure Behavior**: Encouraging and rewarding secure behavior can also contribute to building a strong security culture. Recognition of employees who exhibit good security practices can reinforce the importance of cybersecurity across the organization.

Conclusion

Investing in regular employee training and fostering a culture of security awareness are key defenses against cyber threats in a mainframe-hybrid cloud environment. By empowering employees with the knowledge and tools to recognize and respond to security risks, organizations can significantly reduce the likelihood of breaches caused by human error. This proactive approach to cybersecurity education is a crucial element in safeguarding an organization's digital assets and maintaining the integrity of its IT infrastructure.

Chapter 6: Application Development and Deployment in Hybrid Clouds

In a hybrid cloud environment that integrates mainframes, the development and deployment of applications require special considerations to leverage the strengths of both architectures. This chapter will explore the nuances of developing applications for mainframes, creating cloud-native applications that integrate with mainframes, and effective deployment strategies in such a hybrid setup.

Developing Applications for Mainframes

- **Legacy System Integration**: Understanding and working with legacy systems is crucial when developing applications for mainframes. This involves dealing with older programming languages, databases, and middleware.
- **Performance Optimization**: Mainframe applications often handle high-volume transactions, so performance optimization is key. Developers need to focus on efficient code that maximizes the processing power of mainframes.
- **Scalability and Reliability**: Applications developed for mainframes should be scalable and reliable, taking

advantage of the mainframe's ability to handle large workloads and its high uptime.

Cloud-Native Application Development and its Integration with Mainframes

- **Building Cloud-Native Apps**: Cloud-native applications are designed to leverage cloud computing frameworks. They are built using services that are fully exploited in the cloud, such as microservices, containerization, and serverless architectures.
- **Integration Challenges**: Integrating cloud-native applications with mainframe systems can be challenging due to different architectures and communication protocols. This requires careful planning and the use of integration technologies like APIs, middleware, or messaging systems.
- **Hybrid Architectures**: Developing applications in a way that they can seamlessly interact with both cloud environments and mainframes is essential. This might involve creating APIs or using web services that can communicate with both systems.

Deployment Strategies in a Hybrid Cloud Environment

- **Continuous Integration/Continuous Deployment (CI/CD)**: Implementing CI/CD pipelines can streamline the deployment of applications in a hybrid cloud environment. This approach allows for automatic testing and deployment of applications, improving efficiency and reducing human errors.
- **Automated Testing**: Automated testing is vital in ensuring

that applications work seamlessly across both mainframe and cloud platforms. This includes testing the integration points between the two systems.

- **Deployment Models**: Choosing the right deployment model (e.g., on-premise, cloud, or multi-cloud) based on the application's requirements is crucial. Factors like data sensitivity, workload, and performance requirements should guide this decision.

Conclusion

Application development and deployment in a mainframe-hybrid cloud environment require a balanced approach that combines traditional development practices with modern cloud-native techniques. Developers must navigate the complexities of integrating legacy systems with cloud services while ensuring that applications are performant, reliable, and secure. By adopting effective deployment strategies and leveraging CI/CD pipelines, organizations can enhance the efficiency and agility of their application development processes in a hybrid cloud setup.

6.1. Developing Applications for Mainframes

Developing applications for mainframes entails a unique set of considerations, particularly when it comes to integrating with legacy systems, optimizing performance, and ensuring scalability and reliability. Let's delve into these aspects:

Legacy System Integration

- **Understanding Legacy Environments**: One of the primary challenges in developing applications for mainframes is the need to integrate with legacy systems. This often involves working with older programming languages (like COBOL or PL/I), databases, and middleware that are specific to mainframes.
- **Interoperability**: Ensuring interoperability between new applications and existing legacy systems is crucial. Developers need to be familiar with both the old and new technology stacks and understand how to bridge them effectively.
- **Data Access and Management**: Accessing and managing data within legacy databases and file systems require a thorough understanding of mainframe data formats and storage mechanisms.

Performance Optimization

- **Efficiency in High-Volume Transactions**: Mainframes are typically used for their ability to process high-volume transactions efficiently. Developers should focus on writing code that maximizes the processing capabilities of the mainframe, ensuring quick and efficient transaction processing.
- **Resource Optimization**: This involves optimizing the use of mainframe resources such as CPU, memory, and I/O operations. Efficient utilization of these resources is key to enhancing the application's performance.

Scalability and Reliability

- **Leveraging Mainframe Strengths**: Applications developed for mainframes should be designed to leverage the inherent scalability and reliability of these systems. Mainframes can handle significant increases in workload without compromising on performance, making them ideal for critical business applications.
- **Fault Tolerance and High Availability**: Ensuring that applications are fault-tolerant and maintain high availability is important, given the mission-critical nature of many mainframe applications. This involves designing applications that can handle system failures gracefully and maintain data integrity under all circumstances.

Conclusion

Developing applications for mainframes requires a blend of understanding legacy systems and modern application development practices. Focusing on performance optimization, scalability, and reliability while ensuring seamless integration with legacy components is crucial. As mainframes continue to play a critical role in large-scale enterprise computing, the ability to develop and integrate modern applications with these systems remains an invaluable skill.

Legacy System Integration

Integrating legacy systems in mainframe environments with modern applications poses unique challenges and requires a nuanced approach. This integration is vital for businesses that rely on mainframe technology for critical operations but also want to leverage the advantages of modern application development. Let's explore these key aspects of legacy system integration:

Understanding Legacy Environments

- **Familiarity with Legacy Technologies**: Developers need to have a good understanding of the technologies that underpin legacy systems, which often include older programming languages like COBOL, PL/I, and assembly languages. Familiarity with mainframe operating systems such as z/OS and databases like DB2 is also important.
- **Working with Mature Software**: Legacy systems often run on software that has been in use for decades, making it robust but also complex. Understanding the nuances of these systems, including their strengths and limitations, is crucial for effective integration.

Interoperability

- **Bridging Technology Gaps**: A major aspect of integrating modern applications with legacy mainframe systems is ensuring interoperability. This requires bridging technology gaps between the old (mainframe) and the new (cloud or modern on-premises) environments.

- **Middleware and APIs**: Middleware and APIs can serve as bridges between legacy and modern systems. Middleware can facilitate communication and data exchange, while APIs can provide more direct interaction between new applications and legacy systems.
- **Adapting to Communication Protocols**: Legacy mainframe systems often use different communication protocols compared to modern applications. Developers may need to implement or use adapters that translate these protocols to ensure smooth data exchange.

Data Access and Management

- **Handling Legacy Data Formats**: Legacy mainframes often store data in formats that are not commonly used in modern systems. Developers must understand these formats to access, extract, and manipulate this data effectively.
- **Integration Tools**: Using integration tools that can interact with legacy databases and file systems is essential. This may include ETL (Extract, Transform, Load) tools, database connectors, and data replication solutions.
- **Maintaining Data Integrity**: When accessing and managing data within legacy systems, maintaining data integrity is paramount. This involves ensuring that data transactions are accurate and do not disrupt the stability of the legacy systems.

Conclusion

Legacy system integration in mainframe environments requires a deep understanding of both old and new technologies and an ability to effectively bridge them. By mastering interoperability techniques, understanding legacy data formats, and utilizing appropriate integration tools, developers can successfully integrate legacy mainframe systems with modern applications, thus extending the value and lifespan of these critical systems.

Performance Optimization

Performance optimization in mainframe environments is a critical aspect, especially when these systems handle high-volume transactions. Optimizing the performance of applications running on mainframes not only ensures efficient processing but also maximizes the return on investment for these robust systems. Here are key strategies for performance optimization in mainframe environments:

Efficiency in High-Volume Transactions

- **Optimized Code for Transaction Processing**: Developers should focus on writing efficient code tailored for the mainframe's architecture. This includes optimizing algorithms and data structures to ensure they make the best use of the mainframe's processing capabilities.
- **Parallel Processing Techniques**: Utilizing the mainframe's ability for parallel processing can significantly enhance transaction processing speed. This involves designing applications that can effectively split tasks into parallel jobs to be processed simultaneously.

Resource Optimization

- **CPU Utilization**: Efficient use of the CPU is crucial in mainframe environments. This can involve optimizing CPU-intensive processes and ensuring that the CPU is not idly waiting for I/O operations or other resources.
- **Memory Management**: Effective memory management ensures that applications use the mainframe's memory resources efficiently. This includes optimizing the use of in-memory data and avoiding unnecessary data duplication.
- **I/O Operations Optimization**: I/O operations can often

be a bottleneck in transaction processing. Optimizing these operations involves ensuring data is accessed and stored in an efficient manner, reducing the frequency and volume of I/O operations where possible.

- **Caching Strategies**: Implementing effective caching can reduce the need for frequent data retrieval operations, thereby saving on I/O and processing time. This involves storing frequently accessed data in faster storage for quicker retrieval.

Conclusion

Performance optimization in mainframe environments is all about making the most efficient use of available resources. By focusing on efficient code development, leveraging parallel processing, and optimizing CPU, memory, and I/O operations, developers can significantly enhance the performance of mainframe applications. This not only improves transaction processing speeds but also contributes to the overall reliability and efficiency of the mainframe systems.

Scalability and Reliability

Scalability and reliability are fundamental aspects when developing applications for mainframe environments, particularly given their role in handling mission-critical operations. Mainframes are renowned for their robust performance under heavy workloads and their ability to maintain high levels of availability and data integrity. Let's explore how to effectively leverage these strengths in application development:

Leveraging Mainframe Strengths

- **Design for Scalability**: Applications should be designed to take advantage of the mainframe's inherent scalability. This means they should be able to handle increasing volumes of transactions or data processing without a proportional increase in response times or resource utilization.
- **Efficient Resource Utilization**: Efficient use of the mainframe's resources, such as CPU and memory, is key to scalability. Applications should be optimized to use these resources judiciously, ensuring they can scale up as workload demands increase.

Fault Tolerance and High Availability

- **Building Fault-Tolerant Systems**: Applications should be designed with fault tolerance in mind, meaning they can continue to operate even in the event of a component failure. This involves implementing redundant processes and failover mechanisms.
- **Ensuring High Availability**: High availability is critical, especially for applications that support essential business processes. This can be achieved through redundant system

components, clustering, and rapid failover capabilities in the event of a system failure.

- **Graceful Failure Handling**: It's crucial that applications can handle failures gracefully. This means they should be able to detect issues, switch to backup systems or processes if available, and resume normal operations with minimal disruption.
- **Data Integrity**: Maintaining data integrity in the face of system failures or other issues is paramount. This involves implementing robust data backup and recovery mechanisms, transaction logging, and ensuring that data is consistently in a valid state.

Conclusion

In developing applications for mainframes, leveraging the system's strengths in scalability and reliability is key. By designing applications that are scalable, fault-tolerant, and capable of maintaining high availability and data integrity, developers can ensure that these applications fully harness the power of mainframe technology. These qualities are particularly important for applications that are critical to business operations, where downtime or data loss can have significant consequences.

6.2. Cloud-Native Application Development and its Integration with Mainframes

The integration of cloud-native application development with mainframe systems represents a strategic approach to leveraging the best of both worlds - the agility and scalability of the cloud and the robustness of mainframes. However, this integration presents unique challenges due to the differing architectures and technologies involved. Let's explore how to effectively develop and integrate cloud-native applications with mainframe systems:

Building Cloud-Native Apps

- **Utilizing Cloud Frameworks**: Cloud-native applications are designed specifically for cloud environments, utilizing frameworks and services optimized for the cloud. This often involves architectures based on microservices, which are small, independently deployable modules.
- **Containerization**: Using containerization technologies like Docker and Kubernetes allows applications to be packaged with their dependencies, ensuring consistency across different cloud environments.
- **Serverless Architectures**: Leveraging serverless computing

can further enhance the scalability and efficiency of cloud-native applications, as it allows developers to focus on code rather than on managing servers.

Integration Challenges

- **Architectural Differences**: The mainframe's traditional, monolithic architecture can be quite different from the distributed and dynamic nature of cloud-native applications. Bridging these architectural differences requires careful planning.
- **Communication Protocols**: Mainframes and cloud environments often use different communication protocols. Ensuring effective communication between these systems can involve using middleware or integration platforms that translate or route messages appropriately.
- **Data Format Compatibility**: Ensuring compatibility between the data formats used in mainframes and cloud applications is another challenge. This may require the use of data transformation tools or services.

Hybrid Architectures

- **Creating APIs**: One effective approach to integration is developing APIs that allow cloud-native applications to interact with mainframe systems. RESTful APIs, in particular, can provide a flexible and scalable way to achieve this interaction.
- **Web Services**: Utilizing web services can facilitate the exchange of data and commands between cloud and mainframe systems, allowing applications to leverage the strengths of both environments.

- **Hybrid Cloud Solutions**: Some cloud providers offer hybrid cloud solutions specifically designed to integrate with mainframe systems. These can simplify the process of connecting cloud-native applications with mainframe data and services.

Conclusion

The development and integration of cloud-native applications with mainframes require a thoughtful approach that addresses the inherent differences between these systems. By leveraging modern application architectures like microservices and containerization, and utilizing integration technologies such as APIs and web services, developers can create hybrid architectures that bring together the scalability and flexibility of the cloud with the power and reliability of mainframes. This hybrid approach enables organizations to innovate rapidly while continuing to rely on the proven capabilities of their mainframe systems.

Building Cloud-Native Apps

Building cloud-native applications is a fundamental shift in how software is developed and deployed, leveraging the full capabilities and flexibility of cloud computing. These applications are designed from the ground up to thrive in the cloud environment, using technologies and architectures that maximize the benefits of the cloud. Let's delve into the key aspects of building cloud-native apps:

Utilizing Cloud Frameworks

- **Microservices Architecture**: Cloud-native applications often adopt a microservices architecture, where the application is divided into small, independently deployable services. Each microservice runs a unique process and communicates through a well-defined interface using lightweight APIs.
- **Dynamic and Agile Development**: This approach enables more dynamic and agile development and deployment practices. Microservices can be developed, deployed, and scaled independently, which enhances the overall agility and resilience of applications.

Containerization

- **Packaging Applications**: Containerization technologies like Docker package applications and their dependencies into a single container that is abstract from the host system. This ensures consistency across different cloud environments, as the container includes not just the application, but also its configuration and dependencies.
- **Orchestration with Kubernetes**: Kubernetes is an orchestration system for Docker containers, managing the deployment and scaling of these containers. It handles the

complexity of running containers across a cluster of machines while managing workloads and services.

Serverless Architectures

- **Focus on Code, Not Servers**: Serverless computing, or Function as a Service (FaaS), allows developers to build and deploy applications without having to manage the underlying servers. Developers can focus on writing the application code, while the cloud provider manages the run-time, server and resource allocation.
- **Scalability and Efficiency**: Serverless architectures can scale automatically with demand, both up and down, and you typically pay only for the compute resources you consume. This makes serverless architectures both cost-effective and highly scalable.

Conclusion

Building cloud-native applications involves leveraging modern architectures like microservices, containerization technologies, and serverless computing. This approach enables organizations to create applications that are highly scalable, resilient, and agile, capable of taking full advantage of the cloud environment. By embracing these cloud-native development practices, organizations can accelerate innovation, improve efficiency, and better align with business objectives.

Integration Challenges

Integrating cloud-native applications with traditional mainframe systems presents several challenges due to the fundamental differences in their architectures, communication protocols, and data formats. Successfully navigating these challenges is key to creating a cohesive and efficient hybrid cloud-mainframe environment. Let's explore these integration challenges in more detail:

Architectural Differences

- **Monolithic vs. Distributed Systems**: Mainframes typically operate on a monolithic architecture where applications are often large and interdependent, in contrast to the distributed, modular nature of cloud-native applications. Bridging this gap requires an understanding of how both architectures operate and interact.
- **Integrating Different Architectures**: The integration process might involve decomposing some monolithic mainframe applications into more modular components or building middleware that allows cloud-native applications to interact effectively with monolithic mainframe applications.

Communication Protocols

- **Diverse Protocol Standards**: Mainframes often use older or proprietary communication protocols, which differ significantly from the modern, standard protocols used in cloud environments. This discrepancy can hinder effective communication between the two systems.
- **Middleware and Integration Platforms**: Utilizing middleware or integration platforms can help bridge the

gap in communication protocols. These tools can translate or route messages between the mainframe and cloud systems, ensuring they can communicate effectively despite their inherent differences.

Data Format Compatibility

- **Mismatch in Data Formats**: Data stored and processed in mainframes often uses formats that are not commonly used in cloud environments. This can pose a challenge when trying to share data between mainframe and cloud-based applications.
- **Data Transformation Tools**: To address this, data transformation tools or services can be employed. These tools convert data from mainframe formats to formats that are compatible with cloud-native applications, and vice versa.
- **APIs for Data Exchange**: Creating APIs that can interpret and translate data between the mainframe and cloud applications is another solution. These APIs serve as an intermediary, facilitating the exchange of data in compatible formats.

Conclusion

Successfully integrating cloud-native applications with mainframe systems requires overcoming significant challenges in architecture, communication, and data compatibility. By employing strategies such as architectural adaptation, using middleware for protocol translation, and implementing data transformation tools, organizations can effectively bridge these gaps. This integration is crucial for leveraging the combined strengths of both cloud-native and mainframe technologies, enabling more versatile and powerful IT solutions.

Hybrid Architectures

Hybrid architectures in mainframe and cloud environments represent a strategic approach to IT infrastructure, combining the stability and power of mainframes with the agility and scalability of cloud computing. Developing such architectures involves creating effective communication channels and integration points between these disparate systems. Let's delve into key strategies for building effective hybrid architectures:

Creating APIs

- **Bridging Systems with APIs**: Application Programming Interfaces (APIs) are a crucial element in hybrid architectures. They provide a standardized way for different software components to interact, crucial for integrating mainframe and cloud-native applications.
- **RESTful APIs**: RESTful APIs are particularly effective due to their simplicity, scalability, and stateless nature. They can be used to create flexible and efficient communication interfaces between cloud-native applications and mainframe systems.

Utilizing Web Services

- **Facilitating Data Exchange**: Web services allow different applications to communicate over the internet using standardized protocols such as SOAP (Simple Object Access Protocol) or REST. They can be used to facilitate the exchange of data and commands between cloud-based applications and mainframe systems.
- **Service-Oriented Architecture (SOA)**: Implementing a service-oriented architecture using web services can help encapsulate mainframe functionality into services that can

be easily consumed by cloud-native applications, promoting reusability and modularity.

Hybrid Cloud Solutions

- **Leveraging Cloud Provider Offerings**: Many cloud providers offer specialized hybrid cloud solutions that are designed to work seamlessly with mainframe systems. These solutions often provide tools and services that simplify the integration of cloud-native applications with mainframe data and services.
- **Custom Integration Tools**: Some solutions include custom integration tools that can directly interact with mainframe systems, facilitating data synchronization, workload balancing, and other integration tasks.
- **Managed Services**: Opting for managed services as part of a hybrid cloud solution can reduce the complexity of managing and integrating disparate systems. These services can handle various aspects of integration, maintenance, and support.

Conclusion

Developing a hybrid architecture that effectively integrates mainframe systems with cloud-native applications requires a thoughtful approach that leverages the strengths of both environments. By utilizing APIs, web services, and specialized hybrid cloud solutions, organizations can create a cohesive and efficient IT infrastructure. This infrastructure not only supports existing mainframe applications but also enables the adoption of modern cloud technologies, driving innovation and improving operational flexibility.

6.3. Deployment Strategies in a Hybrid Cloud Environment

Deploying applications in a hybrid cloud environment, which involves both mainframe systems and cloud platforms, requires strategic planning to ensure smooth and efficient operations. The deployment strategy must consider the unique aspects of both environments and leverage modern methodologies like Continuous Integration/Continuous Deployment (CI/CD) and automated testing. Let's explore these deployment strategies:

Continuous Integration/Continuous Deployment (CI/CD)

- **Streamlining Deployment Processes**: Implementing CI/CD pipelines is crucial in a hybrid cloud environment. CI/CD automates the integration and deployment processes, allowing for more frequent and reliable software releases.
- **Automated Build and Testing**: In CI/CD, code changes are automatically built, tested, and prepared for release. This automation significantly reduces the likelihood of human error and ensures that new code integrates seamlessly with existing code.
- **Enhanced Efficiency**: By automating the deployment process, CI/CD pipelines enable faster development cycles and quicker deployment of features, updates, and fixes.

Automated Testing

- **Ensuring Cross-Platform Functionality**: Automated testing is essential to ensure applications function correctly across both mainframe and cloud environments. This is particularly important for applications that rely on interactions between these two platforms.
- **Testing Integration Points**: Special attention should be given to testing the integration points between mainframe and cloud components. Automated tests should cover these interfaces to ensure smooth data exchange and functionality.
- **Regression Testing**: Regular regression testing can be automated to ensure that new updates do not adversely affect existing functionalities in the hybrid environment.

Deployment Models

- **Selecting the Right Model**: Choosing the appropriate deployment model is crucial and should be based on specific application requirements. Options include on-premise (mainframe), cloud-based, or a multi-cloud approach.
- **Considerations for Deployment**: Factors that influence this decision include data sensitivity and compliance requirements, which may necessitate on-premise deployment for certain aspects; workload and scalability requirements, which may favor cloud deployment; and performance considerations.
- **Hybrid Deployment Approach**: In many cases, a hybrid deployment approach may be suitable, where some components are deployed on-premise (such as on

mainframes) and others in the cloud. This approach allows organizations to leverage the strengths of both environments.

Conclusion

Effective deployment strategies in a hybrid cloud environment require a combination of modern development practices like CI/CD, comprehensive automated testing, and careful selection of deployment models. These strategies ensure that applications are deployed efficiently, function reliably across both mainframe and cloud platforms, and meet the diverse needs of the organization. By adopting these approaches, businesses can maximize the benefits of their hybrid cloud-mainframe infrastructure, enhancing agility, scalability, and operational efficiency.

Continuous Integration/Continuous Deployment (CI/CD)

Continuous Integration/Continuous Deployment (CI/CD) is a fundamental methodology in modern software development, especially pertinent in hybrid cloud environments. CI/CD pipelines facilitate a more agile, efficient, and error-resistant development and deployment process. Here's a closer look at how CI/CD benefits hybrid cloud environments:

Streamlining Deployment Processes

- **Automating Integration and Deployment**: Implementing CI/CD pipelines in a hybrid cloud environment automates crucial steps in the software development process. This includes integrating code from different team members, testing, and deploying to various environments (mainframe, cloud, or both).
- **Consistency Across Environments**: With CI/CD, the deployment process becomes consistent across different platforms, whether deploying on mainframes or cloud environments. This consistency is vital for reducing configuration errors and ensuring that applications run smoothly in all environments.

Automated Build and Testing

- **Immediate Integration**: Continuous Integration involves automatically integrating code changes into a main repository. This immediate integration helps in identifying conflicts and issues early in the development cycle.
- **Automated Testing**: CI/CD pipelines typically include automated testing, which verifies that each integration meets the necessary quality standards before deployment. Automated tests can range from unit tests to more

complex integration and performance tests, ensuring that the application works as expected.

- **Error Reduction**: Automated builds and tests significantly reduce the chance of human error, often a primary cause of bugs in software. This automation ensures that errors are detected and corrected as early as possible.

Enhanced Efficiency

- **Faster Development Cycles**: By automating many aspects of the build and deployment process, CI/CD enables faster development cycles. Developers can focus more on writing code and less on the manual processes of integrating and deploying that code.
- **Quicker Feature Releases**: CI/CD allows for quicker and more frequent releases of new features and updates. This responsiveness is particularly beneficial in competitive markets where speed to market can be a crucial differentiator.
- **Immediate Feedback**: The continuous nature of CI/CD provides developers with immediate feedback on their code, allowing for quick corrections and adjustments. This immediate feedback loop improves overall code quality and accelerates the development process.

Conclusion

In a hybrid cloud environment, CI/CD pipelines are essential for streamlining deployment processes, ensuring consistent automated builds and testing, and enhancing overall development efficiency. By adopting CI/CD, organizations can improve their ability to quickly and reliably deliver software across diverse platforms, from traditional mainframes to modern cloud infrastructures. This approach not only speeds up the release cycle but also enhances the quality and reliability of software deployments.

Automated Testing

Automated testing in a hybrid cloud-mainframe environment is pivotal for ensuring that applications function seamlessly across different platforms. It plays a critical role in verifying the integrity and functionality of applications, particularly those that interact between mainframe and cloud environments. Let's delve into the specifics of implementing effective automated testing strategies:

Ensuring Cross-Platform Functionality

- **Comprehensive Testing**: Automated testing must cover all aspects of the application, ensuring it functions correctly in both mainframe and cloud environments. This involves testing under various scenarios and conditions that the application may encounter in each environment.
- **Environment Simulation**: Simulating the different environments in testing phases helps in identifying any platform-specific issues. This ensures that the application behaves as expected in both mainframe and cloud settings.

Testing Integration Points

- **Focus on Interoperability**: Special attention needs to be given to the integration points where the mainframe and cloud components interact. These are critical junctures where data exchange and functionality coordination occur.
- **Interface Testing**: Automated tests should rigorously test these interfaces to ensure that data is correctly transmitted and received, and that all integrated components are working harmoniously.
- **API and Service Testing**: For applications that use APIs or web services to integrate mainframe and cloud components, testing should include validating these APIs

and services for correct functionality, response time, and handling of edge cases.

Regression Testing

- **Automated Regression Suites**: Implementing automated regression testing ensures that new updates or changes to the application do not break existing functionality. This is crucial in a hybrid environment where changes in one part of the system can have cascading effects on other parts.
- **Continuous Regression**: In a CI/CD pipeline, regression tests should be run continuously. This ensures that any issues introduced by new code are identified and addressed as soon as possible.
- **Version Compatibility**: Regression tests should also verify that the application remains compatible with different versions of system components, especially if mainframe systems are not updated as frequently as cloud components.

Conclusion

Automated testing is an indispensable component of developing and maintaining applications in a hybrid cloud-mainframe environment. It ensures that applications are robust, reliable, and functionally consistent across different platforms. By thoroughly testing cross-platform functionality, integration points, and implementing regular regression testing, organizations can maintain high-quality standards and swiftly respond to any issues, thereby ensuring the smooth operation of their hybrid IT infrastructure.

Deployment Models

Selecting the right deployment model in a hybrid cloud-mainframe environment is a strategic decision that significantly impacts the application's performance, scalability, compliance, and overall effectiveness. The decision should align with the specific requirements of the application, as well as the broader goals of the organization. Let's explore the key considerations in choosing the appropriate deployment model:

Selecting the Right Model

- **On-Premise (Mainframe)**: Some applications, particularly those requiring high levels of security or those deeply integrated with legacy systems, might be best suited for on-premise deployment on mainframes.
- **Cloud-Based Deployment**: Cloud deployment is ideal for applications that demand scalability, flexibility, and rapid development. Cloud platforms offer a range of services that can enhance application functionality, such as advanced analytics, artificial intelligence, and machine learning capabilities.
- **Multi-Cloud Approach**: A multi-cloud approach involves deploying applications across multiple cloud environments. This can provide benefits such as avoiding vendor lock-in, optimizing costs, and leveraging the unique strengths of different cloud providers.

Considerations for Deployment

- **Data Sensitivity and Compliance**: For applications handling sensitive data, or those subject to stringent regulatory and compliance requirements, on-premise deployment might be preferable. This allows for greater control over data security and compliance.

- **Workload and Scalability**: Cloud environments are typically better suited for applications with variable workloads or those requiring the ability to scale resources quickly and efficiently.
- **Performance Requirements**: The deployment model should align with the application's performance requirements. Applications requiring high processing power and low latency might benefit from on-premise deployment, while those needing flexibility and high availability might be better suited for the cloud.

Hybrid Deployment Approach

- **Leveraging Both Environments**: A hybrid deployment approach combines on-premise and cloud-based deployment. This model is particularly beneficial for organizations transitioning to the cloud or those that require the strengths of both environments.
- **Balancing Needs**: Hybrid deployment allows for the balancing of computational needs, security requirements, and costs. For instance, an application could use mainframe systems for high-volume transaction processing and the cloud for handling less sensitive tasks or for providing additional services like analytics.
- **Seamless Integration**: Key to a successful hybrid deployment is ensuring seamless integration between on-premise and cloud components. This involves careful planning of the network architecture, data synchronization, and application interoperability.

Conclusion

Choosing the right deployment model in a hybrid cloud-mainframe environment requires a thoughtful analysis of the application's specific needs, regulatory requirements, and the organization's operational goals. Whether opting for on-premise, cloud-based, multi-cloud, or a hybrid approach, the decision should strategically leverage the strengths of each environment to optimize performance, scalability, security, and compliance.

Chapter 7: Mainframe Modernization and Cloud Migration

Mainframe modernization and cloud migration represent critical strategies for organizations looking to leverage new technologies while maintaining the robust functionality of their legacy systems. This chapter delves into the nuances of modernizing mainframes, strategies for migrating mainframe applications to the cloud, and finding the right balance between modernization and preserving essential legacy systems.

The Modernization of Legacy Mainframe Systems

- **Updating Legacy Infrastructure**: Modernization often involves updating the hardware and software of legacy mainframe systems to enhance their performance, security, and compatibility with modern technologies.
- **Incorporating New Technologies**: This can include integrating new technologies such as web services, APIs, and cloud connectivity into the mainframe environment to improve interoperability and flexibility.
- **Refactoring Applications**: Refactoring legacy applications to more modular architectures, like microservices, can make them more adaptable and easier to integrate with

modern cloud-based services.

Strategies for Migrating Mainframe Applications to the Cloud

- **Rehosting (Lift and Shift)**: Rehosting involves moving existing mainframe applications to the cloud without significant modification. This strategy is often the quickest way to migrate but may not take full advantage of cloud-native features.
- **Replatforming**: This involves making some level of optimization to the application to fit into the new cloud environment, such as changing the database to a cloud-native database service.
- **Refactoring/Re-architecting**: This is a more comprehensive approach, where applications are significantly modified or entirely re-architected to become cloud-native. This strategy is more resource-intensive but fully leverages the cloud's capabilities.

Balancing Between Modernization and Preserving Legacy Systems

- **Assessing Business Needs**: It's important to assess which applications should be modernized or migrated to the cloud, and which should remain on mainframes. This decision is often guided by factors like application complexity, performance requirements, and cost.
- **Hybrid Solutions**: In many cases, a hybrid approach that combines maintaining some applications on mainframes while migrating others to the cloud can be effective. This allows organizations to leverage the strengths of both environments.

- **Continuous Evaluation**: Modernization and migration are not one-time events but ongoing processes. Regular evaluation of the IT landscape and business needs can guide further modernization and migration efforts.

Conclusion

Modernizing mainframe systems and migrating applications to the cloud are crucial steps for businesses looking to stay competitive in a rapidly evolving technological landscape. These processes involve careful planning and strategizing to ensure that the unique benefits of mainframes are retained while embracing the flexibility and scalability of cloud computing. By finding the right balance and approach, organizations can optimize their IT infrastructure to be more efficient, agile, and aligned with current and future business needs.

7.1. The Modernization of Legacy Mainframe Systems

The modernization of legacy mainframe systems is a critical step for organizations aiming to keep pace with the rapidly evolving technological landscape while leveraging their existing investments. This process involves not just updating the existing infrastructure but also adapting to newer technologies and approaches to software development. Here's a closer look at these key areas:

Updating Legacy Infrastructure

- **Hardware and Software Upgrades**: Modernizing mainframes often starts with updating the hardware to newer, more powerful models and upgrading the core software, including the operating system and management tools. This enhancement boosts performance, security, and efficiency.
- **Embracing Modern Software Practices**: Updating software also involves adopting modern development practices and tools, which can lead to improved maintainability and functionality of the applications running on mainframes.

Incorporating New Technologies

- **Web Services and APIs**: Integrating web services and APIs enables mainframes to communicate more effectively with other systems, including cloud-based platforms. This integration is key to achieving a seamless flow of data across different environments.
- **Cloud Connectivity**: Establishing cloud connectivity allows for hybrid cloud scenarios where mainframes and cloud environments can complement each other. This can include using cloud resources for certain workloads or data storage.
- **Enhancing Interoperability**: The integration of these new technologies enhances the mainframe's interoperability with modern IT ecosystems, making it a more flexible and valuable asset in the organization's infrastructure.

Refactoring Applications

- **Moving to Modular Architectures**: Refactoring applications to more modular architectures like microservices is a significant step in modernization. This approach breaks down large, monolithic applications into smaller, independent components that are easier to manage, update, and scale.
- **Easier Integration with Modern Services**: Modular applications can more easily interact with cloud-based services and other modern applications, increasing the mainframe's utility and ensuring that it remains a relevant part of the IT infrastructure.
- **Continuous Integration/Continuous Deployment**: Adopting CI/CD practices as part of the refactoring process can further enhance the agility and responsiveness

of mainframe application development and maintenance.

Conclusion

Modernizing legacy mainframe systems is a multifaceted process that involves updating both the hardware and software, integrating new technologies for better interoperability, and refactoring applications to align with modern architectural patterns. Through this modernization, organizations can significantly extend the life and utility of their mainframe investments, making them integral and dynamic components of a modern IT ecosystem.

Updating Legacy Infrastructure

Updating legacy infrastructure, particularly in the context of mainframe systems, is a critical step in modernization efforts. This process not only revitalizes the hardware and software to meet current technological standards but also aligns them with modern development practices and tools. Let's delve into the specifics of this process:

Hardware and Software Upgrades

- **Upgrading Mainframe Hardware**: Modernizing mainframes typically involves upgrading to newer, more powerful models. These newer models offer improved processing capabilities, higher storage capacities, and better energy efficiency. Such upgrades can significantly boost the performance and scalability of mainframe systems.
- **Software Updates**: Alongside hardware, it's essential to upgrade the core software components of the mainframe. This includes the operating system, database management systems, and other critical management tools. Upgrading these software components can enhance security, improve system stability, and introduce new features and capabilities.
- **Ensuring Compatibility**: During the upgrade process, ensuring compatibility between new hardware and existing software, and vice versa, is crucial. Thorough testing should be conducted to ensure that all components of the mainframe work seamlessly together.

Embracing Modern Software Practices

- **Modern Development Tools and Methodologies**: Adopting modern software development practices such as

Agile and DevOps can significantly improve the software development lifecycle on mainframes. These methodologies promote faster development cycles, more efficient workflows, and better collaboration among teams.

- **Integration with Modern Technologies**: Upgrading software also involves integrating modern technologies and platforms with mainframe systems. For instance, incorporating cloud services, containerization, and microservices architecture can make mainframe applications more flexible and easier to integrate with modern IT ecosystems.
- **Continuous Integration/Continuous Deployment (CI/CD)**: Implementing CI/CD pipelines in mainframe development can streamline the process of integrating new code and deploying applications. This approach not only speeds up deployment cycles but also helps in maintaining high code quality and reducing potential deployment errors.

Conclusion

Updating legacy mainframe infrastructure is a multifaceted process involving both hardware and software upgrades. By embracing modern software practices and tools, organizations can significantly enhance the performance, security, and efficiency of their mainframe systems. These upgrades are essential for keeping mainframe systems relevant and effective in today's rapidly evolving technological landscape, enabling them to integrate more seamlessly with contemporary IT architectures and practices.

Incorporating New Technologies

Incorporating new technologies into legacy mainframe systems is a pivotal step in modernization, enhancing their functionality and enabling them to integrate more effectively with current IT ecosystems. This process involves introducing technologies like web services, APIs, and cloud connectivity, which play crucial roles in improving the interoperability and flexibility of mainframe systems. Let's explore these aspects in more detail:

Web Services and APIs

- **Facilitating Communication**: The integration of web services and APIs is essential for enabling mainframes to communicate effectively with other systems, especially modern, cloud-based platforms. This communication is vital for a seamless flow of data across different environments.
- **API Management**: Implementing API management solutions can help in effectively creating, deploying, and monitoring APIs. This ensures that the APIs remain secure, efficient, and reliable for data exchange between mainframes and other systems.

Cloud Connectivity

- **Hybrid Cloud Integration**: Establishing cloud connectivity is key to creating hybrid cloud scenarios, where the robust processing power of mainframes can be effectively paired with the scalability and flexibility of cloud environments.
- **Leveraging Cloud Resources**: This integration allows mainframes to offload certain workloads or utilize cloud resources for storage and enhanced computing capabilities,

leading to optimized overall system performance and cost-efficiency.

- **Cloud Services Integration**: Integrating cloud services can enhance the capabilities of mainframe systems, allowing them to benefit from advancements in areas like artificial intelligence, analytics, and machine learning offered by cloud providers.

Enhancing Interoperability

- **Bridging Technological Gaps**: By incorporating these new technologies, mainframes become more adaptable and interoperable within modern IT infrastructures. This interoperability is crucial for mainframes to remain relevant and functional in a rapidly evolving technological landscape.
- **Modernization Without Replacement**: This approach allows organizations to modernize their mainframe systems without completely replacing them, preserving critical legacy applications while still benefiting from new technological advancements.
- **Strategic Asset Transformation**: The modernization process transforms mainframes from isolated systems to integral, interconnected components of the broader IT ecosystem, enhancing their value and utility within the organization.

Conclusion

Incorporating new technologies such as web services, APIs, and cloud connectivity into mainframe systems is essential for modernization. It not only enhances the mainframe's interoperability with modern IT ecosystems but also transforms it into a more dynamic and flexible asset. This strategic integration allows mainframes to continue playing a vital role in organizational IT infrastructure, leveraging their inherent strengths while embracing the benefits of contemporary technology advancements.

Refactoring Applications

Refactoring applications, especially those running on mainframe systems, into more modern, modular architectures is a crucial aspect of digital transformation. This process not only makes the applications more adaptable and efficient but also aligns them with contemporary software development practices. Let's explore the key facets of refactoring applications in a mainframe environment:

Moving to Modular Architectures

- **From Monolithic to Microservices**: Refactoring often involves transitioning from a monolithic architecture, where the application is a single, indivisible unit, to a microservices architecture. In microservices, the application is divided into smaller, independently deployable services, each responsible for specific functionalities.
- **Benefits of Modularity**: This modularity makes the applications easier to manage, update, and scale. It allows different parts of the application to be developed, deployed, and scaled independently, enhancing overall flexibility and reducing downtime during updates.

Easier Integration with Modern Services

- **Enhancing Interoperability**: Modular applications, particularly when structured as microservices, can more easily interface with cloud-based services and APIs. This interoperability is key for integrating mainframe applications with modern cloud platforms and services.
- **Leveraging Cloud Capabilities**: Through refactoring, mainframe applications can leverage the scalability, resilience, and extensive capabilities of cloud services, such

as data analytics, artificial intelligence, and machine learning.

Continuous Integration/Continuous Deployment

- **Streamlining Development and Deployment**: Implementing Continuous Integration (CI) and Continuous Deployment (CD) as part of the refactoring process aligns mainframe development practices with modern, agile methodologies.
- **Automated Testing and Deployment**: CI/CD introduces automation in the testing and deployment processes, enabling more frequent and reliable updates. This automation is particularly beneficial for mainframe environments, which traditionally have longer development cycles.
- **Enhancing Agility and Responsiveness**: With CI/CD, updates and new features can be developed, tested, and deployed more rapidly and with fewer errors, significantly enhancing the agility and responsiveness of mainframe application development and maintenance.

Conclusion

Refactoring mainframe applications into more modular architectures, such as microservices, and adopting CI/CD practices, represents a significant leap towards modernizing legacy systems. This approach not only improves the manageability and scalability of applications but also ensures their seamless integration with modern cloud-based services and infrastructures. As a result, mainframe systems can continue to be a valuable and integral part of the IT ecosystem, effectively supporting both current and future business needs.

7.2. Strategies for Migrating Mainframe Applications to the Cloud

Migrating mainframe applications to the cloud is a strategic process that involves various approaches, each with its advantages and levels of complexity. The choice of strategy depends on the organization's goals, the specific needs of the application, available resources, and how closely they want to integrate with cloud-native capabilities. Let's explore these strategies:

Rehosting (Lift and Shift)

- **Direct Migration**: Rehosting involves migrating existing mainframe applications to the cloud with little or no modifications. Essentially, it's about lifting the application from the mainframe and shifting it to a cloud environment.
- **Speed and Simplicity**: This approach is often the quickest and least complex way to migrate. It's particularly suitable for organizations looking to migrate rapidly with minimal disruption.
- **Limited Cloud-Native Benefits**: While rehosting is efficient, it may not allow organizations to fully utilize cloud-native features such as scalability, elasticity, and microservices, since the application's core architecture

remains unchanged.

Replatforming

- **Moderate Modifications**: Replatforming involves making some optimizations to the application to better fit the cloud environment. This might include altering the application's data layer to use cloud-native database services or modifying the application to better align with the cloud's scaling capabilities.
- **Balanced Approach**: This strategy strikes a balance between the simplicity of rehosting and the benefits of more extensive cloud-native features. It allows organizations to gain more from cloud capabilities without a complete overhaul of the application.
- **Optimization Without Overhaul**: Replatforming can improve performance and reduce costs while avoiding the complexity and risk of a full-scale refactoring.

Refactoring/Re-architecting

- **Full Transformation**: Refactoring or re-architecting involves significant modifications to the application, essentially rebuilding it to be cloud-native. This might involve adopting microservices architecture, serverless computing, or fully leveraging cloud-based services and APIs.
- **Maximizing Cloud Potential**: This approach allows organizations to fully utilize the capabilities of the cloud, including scalability, resilience, and rapid deployment. It is ideal for applications that require high flexibility and scalability.

- **Resource and Time Intensive**: Refactoring is the most resource-intensive approach. It requires significant time, expertise, and investment but offers the highest degree of integration with cloud capabilities and the best long-term benefits in terms of agility and scalability.

Conclusion

The strategy for migrating mainframe applications to the cloud should align with the organization's broader digital transformation goals. While rehosting offers speed and simplicity, replatforming provides a middle ground, and refactoring offers full cloud-native capabilities. The choice depends on various factors including application complexity, business needs, and the desired level of cloud integration. Each approach has its merits, and in some cases, a combination of strategies may be employed for different applications within the same organization.

Rehosting (Lift and Shift)

Rehosting, commonly known as "Lift and Shift," is a strategy used in migrating mainframe applications to the cloud. This approach has its distinct characteristics and implications, which are important to understand for organizations considering cloud migration. Let's delve into the details of the Rehosting strategy:

Direct Migration

- **Minimal Changes**: Rehosting is characterized by moving existing applications to the cloud with little to no modification to the application code. The application is essentially lifted from its current mainframe environment and shifted to a cloud platform.
- **Preservation of Existing Codebase**: This strategy allows the preservation of the existing codebase and business logic, which can be a significant advantage if the application is stable and well-understood.

Speed and Simplicity

- **Rapid Migration Process**: One of the main advantages of rehosting is the speed of the migration process. Because it involves minimal changes, the migration can typically be accomplished more quickly than other strategies.
- **Reduced Complexity**: The simplicity of this approach reduces the risks and complexities associated with significant code alterations. It's a straightforward process that often requires less planning and fewer resources compared to more complex migration strategies.

Limited Cloud-Native Benefits

- **Not Leveraging Full Cloud Capabilities**: While rehosting is a quick way to migrate to the cloud, it doesn't allow organizations to take full advantage of cloud-native features. The core architecture of the application remains the same, which may limit scalability, elasticity, and the ability to implement modern development practices like microservices.
- **Potential for Increased Costs**: Without optimization for the cloud environment, rehosted applications might not operate as efficiently as they could. This can lead to higher operational costs, particularly in terms of cloud resource usage.
- **Future Modernization Consideration**: Organizations might choose rehosting as a first step in their cloud journey, with plans to further modernize the application in the cloud at a later stage. This staged approach allows for a quicker initial migration but with a roadmap for future optimization and transformation.

Conclusion

Rehosting is a viable strategy for organizations seeking a quick and less complex migration path to the cloud. It's particularly suitable for applications where the primary goal is to migrate with minimal changes and disruption. However, it's important to recognize that this approach may not fully capitalize on the benefits of cloud computing, and future modernization might be necessary to optimize cloud resource usage and gain full cloud-native advantages.

Replatforming

Replatforming is a strategic approach for migrating mainframe applications to the cloud, involving moderate modifications to enhance compatibility with cloud environments. This strategy aims to strike a balance between minimizing changes to the application and leveraging some of the key benefits of cloud computing. Let's explore the aspects of replatforming in more detail:

Moderate Modifications

- **Targeted Changes**: Unlike rehosting, replatforming involves making thoughtful, specific changes to the application to better fit it into the cloud environment. This could include updating or replacing certain components of the application rather than altering its core architecture.
- **Utilizing Cloud-Native Services**: A common replatforming strategy is to modify the application's data layer to utilize cloud-native database services. This can significantly improve data handling efficiency and scalability in the cloud.

Balanced Approach

- **Leveraging Cloud Features**: Replatforming allows an application to take advantage of certain cloud-native features such as improved scalability, enhanced performance, and sometimes reduced costs, without the need for a complete re-architecture.
- **Reduced Complexity**: This approach provides a middle ground between the simplicity of rehosting (lift and shift) and the complexity of full refactoring or re-architecting. It's particularly suitable for applications that can benefit from some cloud features but do not require a complete transformation to be effective.

Optimization Without Overhaul

- **Performance Improvements**: By making selective modifications, replatforming can lead to improved performance in the cloud. For instance, leveraging auto-scaling features of the cloud can enhance the application's responsiveness to varying workloads.
- **Cost-Effective Approach**: Replatforming can be more cost-effective than a full re-architecting. It allows organizations to optimize cloud resource usage without the substantial investment of time and resources required for a complete overhaul.
- **Risk Mitigation**: This approach also mitigates the risks associated with extensive code changes, as it focuses on optimizations rather than a complete rebuild. It's a pragmatic approach for applications where extensive modifications are unnecessary or not feasible due to budget or time constraints.

Conclusion

Replatforming represents a strategic approach to cloud migration, offering a way to optimize and enhance applications for the cloud without the need for extensive redevelopment. It is an effective strategy for organizations looking to modernize their applications with a balanced investment in time, cost, and effort, allowing them to leverage cloud capabilities while maintaining the core functionality of their existing applications.

Refactoring/Re-architecting

Refactoring or re-architecting mainframe applications for the cloud is a comprehensive approach that involves a full-scale transformation of the application to be cloud-native. This strategy is the most intensive in terms of resources and effort but offers substantial long-term benefits by fully leveraging the cloud's capabilities. Let's delve into the specifics:

Full Transformation

- **Rebuilding for Cloud-Native**: Refactoring involves fundamentally rethinking how the application is structured and how it operates. This typically means breaking down a monolithic application into a microservices architecture, where each service is loosely coupled and can be developed, deployed, and scaled independently.
- **Adopting Advanced Cloud Features**: During the refactoring process, applications might be redesigned to utilize serverless computing models, which can significantly improve scalability and operational efficiency. The use of cloud-based services and APIs is also integral to this approach, allowing for more agile development and operation.

Maximizing Cloud Potential

- **Leveraging Full Range of Cloud Benefits**: By transforming applications to be cloud-native, organizations can fully exploit cloud features such as auto-scaling, distributed computing, and advanced cloud services like AI and data analytics. This maximizes the potential benefits of cloud computing in terms of performance, scalability, and resilience.
- **Ideal for Dynamic Applications**: Refactoring is particularly well-suited for applications that need high levels of flexibility and scalability, such as those experiencing variable or rapidly growing demand.

Resource and Time Intensive

- **Significant Investment Required**: Refactoring is the most resource-intensive migration strategy. It demands substantial time, technical expertise, and financial investment. The process involves not just technical changes but often a shift in the development culture and methodology.
- **Long-Term Payoffs**: Despite the initial investment, refactoring offers the highest degree of integration with cloud capabilities. In the long term, this can result in greater agility, scalability, and potential cost savings, as well as the ability to stay current with technological advancements.
- **Continuous Improvement and Adaptation**: Once refactored, applications are generally easier to update and improve over time, aligning with the principles of continuous integration and continuous deployment, which are pivotal in modern software development practices.

Conclusion

Refactoring or re-architecting applications for the cloud is a strategic choice for organizations looking to fully embrace cloud computing's advantages. While this approach requires significant resources and a commitment to a substantial transformation process, it ultimately leads to applications that are more flexible, scalable, and aligned with modern technological capabilities. For organizations prioritizing long-term agility and innovation, refactoring presents a compelling path forward in their cloud migration journey.

7.3. Balancing Between Modernization and Preserving Legacy Systems

Balancing the modernization of IT infrastructure with the preservation of legacy mainframe systems is a critical challenge for many organizations. This balance requires a strategic approach to determine which applications are best suited for modernization or migration to the cloud, and which should continue to reside on mainframes. Let's explore how organizations can navigate this balance:

Assessing Business Needs

- **Analyzing Application Suitability**: Not all applications are ideal candidates for cloud migration or modernization. An assessment should be made based on the application's complexity, the specific business needs it serves, its performance requirements, and the costs involved in migrating or modernizing it.
- **Risk and Benefit Analysis**: Consider the risks, such as potential downtime and data integrity issues, against the benefits of modernization, like increased flexibility and efficiency. This analysis helps in making informed decisions about which systems to modernize.

Hybrid Solutions

- **Combining Mainframe and Cloud Strengths**: A hybrid approach, where some applications remain on the mainframe while others are migrated to the cloud, can be an effective strategy. This allows organizations to capitalize on the mainframe's reliability and security for certain critical applications, while leveraging the cloud's scalability and innovation for others.
- **Integration of Environments**: In a hybrid model, it's crucial to ensure seamless integration and communication between cloud-based and mainframe applications. This may involve the use of middleware, APIs, or other integration technologies.

Continuous Evaluation

- **Ongoing Modernization Process**: Modernization and migration should be viewed as continuous processes rather than one-time projects. The IT landscape and business needs are constantly evolving, and strategies should adapt accordingly.
- **Regular Review and Adaptation**: Regularly reviewing the performance, costs, and alignment of IT infrastructure with business objectives is essential. This helps in identifying new opportunities for modernization or different approaches to managing legacy systems.
- **Staying Agile and Responsive**: The ability to quickly adapt to new technologies and market demands is crucial in today's dynamic business environment. Continuous evaluation supports an agile and responsive IT strategy, ensuring the organization remains competitive and

efficient.

Conclusion

Balancing modernization with the preservation of legacy systems requires a thoughtful approach that carefully assesses business needs and leverages the strengths of both modern and legacy technologies. A hybrid approach often serves as a practical solution, providing flexibility and ensuring continuity of critical business operations. Regular evaluation and adaptation of the IT strategy are key to maintaining this balance, ensuring that the organization's technology infrastructure effectively supports its evolving needs and goals.

Assessing Business Needs

Assessing business needs is a critical step in the decision-making process regarding the modernization or migration of applications to the cloud. This assessment requires a comprehensive understanding of each application's role, functionality, and the potential impact of modernization on the business. Here's how organizations can approach this assessment:

Analyzing Application Suitability

- **Understanding Application Complexity**: The complexity of an application, including its integration with other systems and dependencies, plays a significant role in determining its suitability for cloud migration or modernization. Complex applications might require a more cautious approach.
- **Aligning with Business Objectives**: The decision should align with the organization's overall business objectives. Applications that are critical to business operations or provide a competitive advantage might be prioritized for modernization.
- **Performance Requirements**: Consider how the application's performance requirements will be met in a modernized environment. Will the cloud offer improved performance, or are there specific requirements that are better served by the existing mainframe setup?
- **Cost Analysis**: Evaluate the costs involved in migrating or modernizing the application, including the costs of potential disruptions during the transition. Compare these against the long-term operational savings and efficiencies that modernization might offer.

Risk and Benefit Analysis

- **Assessing Potential Risks**: Identify potential risks associated with modernizing each application, such as downtime during migration, data loss, or security vulnerabilities. How these risks are mitigated will be crucial in the decision-making process.
- **Balancing Risks with Benefits**: Weigh the identified risks against the potential benefits of modernization, such as increased agility, scalability, and the ability to leverage advanced cloud services. Benefits also include long-term cost savings and improved alignment with modern IT practices.
- **Business Continuity Considerations**: Consider the impact of modernization on business continuity. Ensure that there are plans in place to maintain operations during the transition and that any potential downtime is acceptable within the context of the business's operational requirements.

Conclusion

Assessing business needs for modernization and cloud migration involves a careful examination of application suitability, a thorough risk-benefit analysis, and an alignment with broader business objectives. This process is essential for making informed decisions that balance the need for technological advancement with the practical realities of business operations. By conducting this assessment, organizations can strategically prioritize which applications to modernize, ensuring that their IT infrastructure effectively supports their current and future business needs.

Hybrid Solutions

Hybrid solutions offer a strategic approach to integrating the robustness of mainframe systems with the agility and scalability of cloud computing. This approach allows organizations to optimize their IT infrastructure by leveraging the unique strengths of both environments. Here's a closer look at implementing hybrid solutions:

Combining Mainframe and Cloud Strengths

- **Leveraging Mainframe Reliability**: For many critical applications, especially those requiring high levels of security and stable performance, mainframes are an ideal environment. Maintaining these applications on the mainframe can capitalize on its proven reliability and security features.
- **Utilizing Cloud Scalability**: The cloud provides scalability and flexibility, which is beneficial for applications that experience variable workloads or require rapid scaling. Migrating such applications to the cloud can improve operational efficiency and reduce costs.
- **Balanced Infrastructure**: By keeping some applications on mainframes and moving others to the cloud, organizations can create a balanced infrastructure that aligns with their specific operational needs and strategic objectives.

Integration of Environments

- **Seamless Application Integration**: A critical aspect of a hybrid approach is ensuring seamless integration between mainframe and cloud applications. This integration is essential for the smooth operation of interconnected systems and services.
- **Middleware Solutions**: Middleware can play a crucial role in bridging the gap between mainframe and cloud environments. It can facilitate data exchange, manage transactions, and ensure consistent communication across different platforms.

- **APIs for Connectivity**: APIs are another vital tool for integration. They provide a standardized method for different applications and services to communicate and share data, regardless of the underlying platform.
- **Consistent Data Management**: Ensuring consistent data management across both environments is important. This may involve data synchronization strategies and robust data governance practices to maintain data integrity and compliance.

Conclusion

Hybrid solutions represent a pragmatic and effective approach to modernizing IT infrastructure. By combining the reliability and security of mainframes with the scalability and innovation of the cloud, organizations can create a versatile and efficient IT ecosystem. Key to the success of this approach is the seamless integration of the two environments, facilitated by middleware, APIs, and strategic data management practices. This integrated approach allows businesses to harness the full potential of their IT assets, enabling them to respond more effectively to evolving business needs and technological advancements.

Continuous Evaluation

Continuous evaluation is a key component in the lifecycle of IT modernization and migration, especially in environments that blend legacy systems with newer cloud technologies. This approach ensures that the IT infrastructure not only meets current business needs but is also poised to adapt to future demands and technological advancements. Let's delve into the importance and implementation of continuous evaluation:

Ongoing Modernization Process

- **Dynamic IT Landscape**: The field of technology is dynamic, with new advancements and tools emerging regularly. Modernization and migration are ongoing processes that should evolve with these technological changes.
- **Aligning with Business Evolution**: As business needs evolve, so too should the IT infrastructure. Continuous modernization ensures that IT capabilities align with and support the changing demands and objectives of the business.

Regular Review and Adaptation

- **Performance Monitoring**: Regularly assessing the performance of both legacy and modernized systems is crucial. This involves monitoring for efficiency, speed, and reliability, ensuring that the systems are operating optimally.
- **Cost-Benefit Analysis**: Continual review of the costs associated with maintaining, upgrading, and operating IT infrastructure is necessary. This includes evaluating the return on investment of modernization efforts and re-

aligning strategies to optimize costs.
- **Alignment with Business Goals**: IT infrastructure should be in constant alignment with the overall business strategy. Regular reviews can help in identifying areas where the IT infrastructure is not fully supporting business goals and requires adaptation.

Staying Agile and Responsive

- **Adapting to Market Changes**: The ability to quickly respond to market changes and new technological opportunities is crucial for maintaining a competitive edge. A continuous evaluation process ensures that an organization's IT infrastructure can quickly adapt to these changes.
- **Agility in IT Decision Making**: Continuous evaluation fosters an agile approach to IT decision-making, allowing for swift responses to emerging challenges and opportunities. This agility is key in leveraging new technologies and methodologies that can enhance business operations.
- **Proactive Rather Than Reactive**: Adopting a proactive stance in IT strategy, as opposed to being reactive, positions an organization to capitalize on technological advancements and stay ahead of potential challenges.

Conclusion

Continuous evaluation is essential in the modern IT landscape, where technology and business needs are perpetually evolving. By regularly assessing and adapting IT infrastructure and strategies, organizations can ensure that their systems remain efficient, cost-effective, and aligned with their business objectives. This ongoing process supports a responsive and agile IT strategy, enabling organizations to swiftly adapt to new technologies and market demands, thereby maintaining their competitiveness and operational efficiency.

Chapter 8: Performance Monitoring and Optimization in Hybrid Clouds

In hybrid cloud environments that incorporate both mainframes and cloud systems, effective performance monitoring and optimization are crucial for ensuring system efficiency and reliability. This chapter will explore the tools and techniques for monitoring performance in such environments, strategies for optimization, and the balancing of workloads to leverage the strengths of both mainframes and cloud infrastructure.

Monitoring Tools and Techniques for Mainframes and Cloud Systems

- **Integrated Monitoring Solutions**: Utilize monitoring tools that offer integrated solutions capable of tracking performance across both mainframes and cloud environments. These tools should provide comprehensive visibility into all aspects of the infrastructure.
- **Real-Time Analytics**: Implement real-time monitoring and analytics to quickly identify and address performance bottlenecks or anomalies. This involves analyzing metrics like CPU usage, memory consumption, network

throughput, and application response times.

- **Predictive Analytics**: Employ predictive analytics to anticipate potential performance issues before they impact operations. This can be based on historical data and usage patterns.

Performance Optimization in Hybrid Environments

- **Resource Allocation Optimization**: Regularly assess and optimize the allocation of resources such as compute, storage, and network bandwidth to ensure they are being used efficiently across both mainframes and cloud systems.
- **Application Performance Management (APM)**: Use APM tools to monitor and manage application performance and ensure that applications are running optimally in the hybrid environment.
- **Automated Scaling**: Implement automated scaling in cloud environments to dynamically adjust resources in response to changing demand, ensuring optimal performance without over-provisioning.

Balancing Workloads Between Mainframes and Cloud Infrastructure

- **Workload Assessment and Distribution**: Assess the nature of workloads and strategically distribute them between mainframes and cloud systems based on their characteristics. For example, high-volume transaction processing might be more suited to mainframes, while flexible, scalable workloads can be allocated to the cloud.
- **Hybrid Cloud Management Platforms**: Use hybrid cloud management platforms to seamlessly move workloads

between mainframes and cloud environments, based on performance, cost, and availability considerations.

- **Continuous Balancing and Optimization**: Regularly review workload distribution to ensure it remains aligned with changing business needs and technology capabilities. Adjust strategies as needed for optimal performance and efficiency.

Conclusion

Performance monitoring and optimization in hybrid cloud environments require a comprehensive approach that includes the use of sophisticated tools and techniques, regular assessment and optimization of resources, and strategic workload balancing. By effectively monitoring and managing the performance of both mainframe and cloud systems, organizations can ensure that their hybrid infrastructure operates efficiently, reliably, and cost-effectively, supporting their operational goals and adapting to evolving business needs.

8.1. Monitoring Tools and Techniques for Mainframes and Cloud Systems

Effective performance monitoring in hybrid cloud environments, which combine mainframe and cloud systems, is crucial for maintaining optimal operation and efficiency. Utilizing advanced monitoring tools and techniques is essential for comprehensive oversight of these diverse systems. Here's how organizations can approach this:

Integrated Monitoring Solutions

- **Unified Monitoring Platform**: Choose monitoring tools that provide an integrated platform capable of overseeing both mainframe and cloud components. This integration is key for a holistic view of the entire IT infrastructure.
- **Comprehensive Visibility**: These tools should offer comprehensive visibility into various aspects of the infrastructure, including hardware health, software performance, and network status across both mainframe and cloud environments.
- **Dashboard and Reporting Features**: The ideal monitoring solution should include customizable dashboards and reporting features, enabling IT teams to

quickly assess system health and performance metrics in a user-friendly manner.

Real-Time Analytics

- **Immediate Performance Insights**: Implement real-time monitoring to provide immediate insights into system performance. This includes tracking metrics such as CPU usage, memory consumption, storage I/O operations, and network throughput.
- **Identifying Bottlenecks**: Real-time analytics help in quickly identifying performance bottlenecks or operational anomalies, enabling prompt corrective actions to maintain system performance and availability.
- **Application Monitoring**: Alongside infrastructure monitoring, focus on application-level metrics like response times and transaction rates to ensure applications are performing optimally in the hybrid environment.

Predictive Analytics

- **Anticipating Future Issues**: Employ predictive analytics to forecast potential performance issues based on historical data and usage patterns. This proactive approach can prevent problems before they impact operations.
- **Capacity Planning**: Use predictive analytics for capacity planning, helping to predict future resource requirements and optimize resource allocation proactively.
- **Automated Alerts and Responses**: Integrate automated alerting systems that notify administrators of predicted performance degradations or potential system failures, and where possible, implement automated responses to

preemptively address these issues.

Conclusion

Monitoring tools and techniques in hybrid cloud environments must be capable of providing integrated, real-time, and predictive insights into both mainframe and cloud systems. By utilizing advanced monitoring solutions, organizations can ensure that they have comprehensive visibility and control over their infrastructure. This level of oversight is crucial for maintaining the performance, reliability, and efficiency of hybrid IT environments, enabling businesses to respond swiftly to changing needs and challenges.

Integrated Monitoring Solutions

Integrated monitoring solutions are essential in managing and optimizing hybrid cloud environments that combine mainframe and cloud systems. A unified approach to monitoring provides a comprehensive view of the entire infrastructure, enabling IT teams to effectively manage and optimize performance. Here's a detailed look at key features of integrated monitoring solutions:

Unified Monitoring Platform

- **Holistic Infrastructure Oversight**: An integrated monitoring platform should provide a unified view of both mainframe and cloud components. This holistic approach is crucial for managing complex hybrid environments effectively.
- **Cross-Platform Compatibility**: The platform should seamlessly integrate with various technologies and platforms, providing consistent monitoring capabilities across different systems, whether they are on-premises mainframes or cloud-based services.

Comprehensive Visibility

- **In-Depth Infrastructure Insights**: The monitoring tool should offer in-depth visibility into all infrastructure layers. This includes real-time monitoring of hardware health (like CPU, memory, and storage utilization), software performance (such as application response times and transaction rates), and network status (including bandwidth usage and latency).
- **Correlation and Analysis**: The ability to correlate data from different sources and analyze it for insights is crucial. This helps in identifying underlying issues that might affect

multiple components of the hybrid infrastructure.

Dashboard and Reporting Features

- **Customizable Dashboards**: Customizable dashboards are vital for tailoring the monitoring interface to meet the specific needs of different teams. Dashboards should provide a real-time overview of the system's health and performance, highlighting critical metrics and alerts.
- **Intuitive Reporting Tools**: The solution should include intuitive reporting tools that allow for the generation of detailed reports. These reports can be used for deeper analysis, historical performance tracking, and informing strategic decisions.
- **Alerting Mechanisms**: Effective alerting mechanisms that notify IT staff of potential issues or deviations from normal performance are essential. This enables prompt responses to prevent or mitigate potential impacts on operations.

Conclusion

Integrated monitoring solutions in hybrid cloud environments enable IT teams to maintain a comprehensive and unified view of their infrastructure, ensuring efficient operation and timely response to issues. By providing deep visibility, customizable dashboards, and effective reporting tools, these solutions are integral to the proactive management and optimization of complex IT environments, combining the robustness of mainframes with the agility of cloud computing.

Real-Time Analytics

Real-time analytics is a vital component in the management of hybrid cloud environments, particularly for ensuring optimal performance and quickly addressing any issues that arise. Here's a closer look at the key aspects of implementing real-time analytics:

Immediate Performance Insights

- **Continuous Monitoring**: Implement a continuous, real-time monitoring system that tracks and analyzes key performance metrics across both mainframe and cloud components. This includes monitoring CPU usage, memory consumption, storage input/output operations, and network throughput.
- **Visualizing Data**: Utilize tools that provide real-time visualization of these metrics. Dashboards that update in real time can offer immediate insights into the health and performance of the entire system.

Identifying Bottlenecks

- **Quick Issue Detection**: Real-time analytics are crucial for quickly identifying any performance bottlenecks or operational anomalies. By monitoring system performance continuously, issues can be detected as they occur, allowing for prompt intervention.
- **Root Cause Analysis**: Use real-time data to perform root cause analysis of performance issues. This can involve correlating different metrics to identify underlying causes of bottlenecks or failures.
- **Proactive Management**: With immediate detection and analysis, IT teams can proactively manage system performance, addressing potential issues before they escalate into more significant problems.

Application Monitoring

- **Tracking Application Performance**: In addition to infrastructure monitoring, it's important to monitor application-level metrics. This includes tracking response times, transaction rates, and other application-specific metrics.
- **End-User Experience Monitoring**: Monitoring the performance from an end-user perspective can provide insights into how application performance is impacting user experience, which is crucial for customer-facing applications.
- **Optimizing Application Workloads**: Real-time analytics can help in optimizing application workloads across the hybrid environment. This could involve shifting workloads or resources based on performance data to ensure optimal operation.

Conclusion

Real-time analytics plays a critical role in the effective management of hybrid cloud environments. By providing immediate insights into system and application performance, identifying bottlenecks, and enabling proactive management, real-time analytics help ensure that both mainframe and cloud components of the infrastructure are functioning optimally. This level of monitoring is essential for maintaining high performance, availability, and a positive user experience in today's complex IT landscapes.

Predictive Analytics

Predictive analytics is increasingly becoming a crucial tool in managing and optimizing hybrid cloud environments. By analyzing historical data and identifying patterns, predictive analytics can forecast future performance issues and resource needs, allowing for proactive management of the IT infrastructure. Here's a detailed look at how predictive analytics can be effectively utilized:

Anticipating Future Issues

- **Proactive Problem Prevention**: Predictive analytics tools analyze historical performance data to identify trends and patterns that may indicate future performance issues or system failures. By predicting these issues before they occur, organizations can take preemptive action to avoid or mitigate them.
- **Pattern Recognition and Analysis**: These tools use advanced algorithms and machine learning techniques to recognize and analyze patterns in data, such as repeated spikes in CPU usage or memory leaks, which could lead to performance degradation or system outages.

Capacity Planning

- **Predicting Resource Needs**: Predictive analytics plays a key role in capacity planning. It can forecast future resource requirements based on historical usage trends and patterns, helping organizations to optimize their resource allocation.
- **Resource Optimization**: By accurately predicting future demands, organizations can ensure that they have the necessary resources available when needed, without over-provisioning or underutilizing their infrastructure, thus

optimizing costs and performance.

- **Demand Forecasting**: This is particularly important in cloud environments, where resources can be scaled dynamically. Predictive analytics helps in understanding when to scale resources up or down.

Automated Alerts and Responses

- **Early Warning Systems**: Integrating predictive analytics with automated alerting systems provides an early warning mechanism for potential issues. These systems can alert administrators to predicted performance degradations or system failures, allowing for rapid response.
- **Automating Preventive Actions**: Where possible, implementing automated responses can significantly enhance system resilience. For instance, if a potential overload is predicted, the system could automatically initiate processes to redistribute workloads or allocate additional resources.
- **Enhancing System Reliability**: The combination of predictive analytics and automated responses not only enhances system reliability but also reduces the burden on IT staff, allowing them to focus on more strategic tasks.

Conclusion

Predictive analytics is a powerful tool in the management of hybrid cloud environments, offering capabilities to anticipate future issues, optimize capacity planning, and automate alerts and responses. By effectively utilizing predictive analytics, organizations can proactively manage their IT infrastructure, ensuring high performance, cost efficiency, and reliability. This proactive approach is key to maintaining a robust and agile IT environment in an increasingly complex and dynamic technological landscape.

8.2. Performance Optimization in Hybrid Environments

Performance optimization in hybrid cloud environments, which include both mainframes and cloud systems, is crucial for ensuring efficient operation and maximizing the benefits of both platforms. Effective resource management, application performance monitoring, and automated scaling are key strategies to achieve this optimization. Let's explore these strategies in more detail:

Resource Allocation Optimization

- **Efficient Use of Resources**: It's essential to regularly assess and fine-tune the allocation of resources, such as computing power, storage, and network bandwidth, to ensure they are being utilized efficiently in both mainframe and cloud environments.
- **Balancing Load Across Platforms**: Distribute workloads in a manner that leverages the strengths of both mainframes and cloud systems. For example, mainframes can handle high-volume transaction processing, while cloud systems can manage scalable, variable workloads.
- **Monitoring Utilization**: Continuous monitoring of resource utilization helps in identifying underused or overused resources, allowing for timely adjustments to

optimize performance and reduce costs.

Application Performance Management (APM)

- **Monitoring Application Health**: Use APM tools to continuously monitor the health and performance of applications running in the hybrid environment. This includes tracking metrics like response time, error rates, and transaction volumes.
- **Identifying Performance Bottlenecks**: APM tools can help in pinpointing performance bottlenecks within applications, whether they are running on mainframes or in the cloud. This information is crucial for targeted optimization efforts.
- **End-User Experience Monitoring**: Ensuring a positive end-user experience is critical. APM tools can provide insights into how application performance impacts the user experience, enabling optimizations that improve user satisfaction.

Automated Scaling

- **Dynamic Resource Adjustment**: Implement automated scaling in cloud environments to dynamically adjust computing resources in response to fluctuating demand. This ensures that applications have the resources they need during peak times without wasting resources during periods of low demand.
- **Cost-Efficiency**: Automated scaling helps in optimizing costs by reducing the need for over-provisioning. Pay-for-use models in cloud environments mean that efficient scaling can directly lead to cost savings.

- **Elasticity and Responsiveness**: This approach enhances the elasticity and responsiveness of cloud-deployed applications, allowing them to quickly adapt to changing usage patterns, which is crucial for maintaining high performance and availability.

Conclusion

Optimizing performance in hybrid cloud environments requires a strategic approach to resource allocation, application performance management, and automated scaling. By effectively managing resources, continuously monitoring and optimizing application performance, and implementing automated scaling in cloud environments, organizations can ensure that their hybrid infrastructure operates at peak efficiency. This optimization is key to leveraging the combined strengths of mainframe and cloud technologies, enabling businesses to achieve high performance, cost efficiency, and an excellent user experience.

Resource Allocation Optimization

Optimizing resource allocation in hybrid environments that encompass both mainframes and cloud systems is crucial for maximizing efficiency and performance. Effective management of resources across these platforms involves careful assessment, strategic distribution of workloads, and ongoing monitoring. Let's delve into these strategies:

Efficient Use of Resources

- **Regular Assessment and Tuning**: Periodically evaluate how resources are allocated across your mainframe and cloud environments. Adjustments might be needed to align with changing demands or to improve efficiency.
- **Optimizing Compute Resources**: Ensure that the computing power in both environments is used efficiently. This might involve scaling resources up or down in the cloud or reallocating tasks on the mainframe to optimize performance.
- **Storage and Network Optimization**: Regularly assess storage use and network bandwidth to ensure they are not bottlenecks. Optimize data storage and transfer processes to prevent unnecessary strain on network and storage resources.

Balancing Load Across Platforms

- **Workload Analysis**: Understand the characteristics of different workloads and identify which platform is best suited for each. Some workloads may require the high-processing power and stability of mainframes, while others might benefit from the cloud's scalability and flexibility.
- **Leveraging Platform Strengths**: Utilize the mainframe

for tasks it excels at, such as high-volume transaction processing or running large, complex batch jobs. Use cloud systems for workloads that are more dynamic or require rapid scalability.

- **Distributing Workloads Strategically**: Distribute workloads to balance the load across platforms, reducing the risk of overburdening a single system and improving overall efficiency.

Monitoring Utilization

- **Continuous Resource Monitoring**: Implement tools and systems to continuously monitor resource utilization in both mainframe and cloud environments. This should include tracking CPU usage, memory usage, storage capacity, and network bandwidth.
- **Identifying Inefficiencies**: Use monitoring data to identify inefficiencies, such as underutilized resources that can be scaled down or overutilized resources that may need additional capacity.
- **Proactive Adjustments**: Be proactive in making adjustments based on monitoring data. This might involve reallocating resources, adjusting workload distribution, or scaling cloud resources to meet current demands.

Conclusion

Effective resource allocation optimization in hybrid environments is key to maximizing the benefits of both mainframes and cloud systems. It requires a careful balance, regular assessment, and strategic workload distribution, underpinned by continuous monitoring of resource utilization. By optimizing how resources are allocated and used, organizations can enhance performance, reduce costs, and ensure their IT infrastructure is fully aligned with their operational needs and objectives.

Application Performance Management (APM)

Application Performance Management (APM) is essential in hybrid cloud environments, ensuring that applications perform optimally across both mainframes and cloud systems. APM tools offer insights into application health and user experience, helping to identify and resolve performance issues. Let's explore the key aspects of APM in a hybrid environment:

Monitoring Application Health

- **Comprehensive Performance Tracking**: Implement APM tools to continuously monitor key performance metrics of applications. This includes tracking response times, error rates, and transaction volumes, which are critical indicators of application health.
- **Real-Time Visibility**: Ensure that the APM tools provide real-time visibility into application performance. This enables quick detection and resolution of issues, minimizing downtime or performance degradation.
- **Cross-Environment Monitoring**: Since applications in hybrid environments might span across mainframes and cloud platforms, APM tools should be capable of monitoring across these different environments seamlessly.

Identifying Performance Bottlenecks

- **Pinpointing Issues**: APM tools can analyze performance data to identify bottlenecks or inefficiencies within applications. This might include issues like slow database queries, memory leaks, or resource contention.
- **Root Cause Analysis**: Advanced APM solutions can assist in root cause analysis, helping to determine whether issues originate in the application code, infrastructure, or

network.

- **Targeted Optimization**: By accurately identifying the sources of performance issues, IT teams can undertake targeted optimization efforts, rather than making broad, less effective changes.

End-User Experience Monitoring

- **User Experience Insights**: Monitor the end-user experience to understand how application performance impacts users. This is particularly important for customer-facing applications where user satisfaction is directly linked to business outcomes.
- **Synthetic and Real User Monitoring**: Utilize both synthetic monitoring (simulating user interactions) and real user monitoring (tracking actual user interactions) to get a comprehensive view of the user experience.
- **Performance Impact Analysis**: Analyze how performance issues affect users, such as increased page load times or transaction failures, and prioritize fixes based on their impact on the user experience.

Conclusion

Effective Application Performance Management in hybrid cloud environments is critical for ensuring that applications perform well and provide a positive user experience. By continuously monitoring application health, identifying performance bottlenecks, and focusing on the end-user experience, organizations can maintain high-performing, reliable applications. APM tools play a vital role in this process, offering the insights and analytics necessary to drive informed optimization efforts, ultimately contributing to the overall success of the organization's digital initiatives.

Automated Scaling

Automated scaling is a key feature of cloud computing that significantly enhances the management of resources in hybrid environments, ensuring applications perform optimally under varying loads. This approach dynamically adjusts resources to meet demand, offering both cost-efficiency and improved application responsiveness. Let's delve into the details of implementing automated scaling in hybrid clouds:

Dynamic Resource Adjustment

- **Adapting to Demand Fluctuations**: Implement automated scaling mechanisms that allow cloud resources to be dynamically adjusted in response to changing demand. During peak usage times, resources are automatically scaled up to meet increased demand, and scaled down during low-usage periods to conserve resources.
- **Real-Time Resource Management**: This dynamic adjustment is typically managed in real-time, ensuring that applications always have access to the resources they need for optimal performance.

Cost-Efficiency

- **Optimizing Resource Utilization**: Automated scaling helps in optimizing resource utilization, which is crucial for cost management in cloud environments. By scaling resources based on actual demand, it eliminates the need for over-provisioning and underutilization.
- **Pay-for-Use Benefits**: In cloud environments, the pay-for-use model means that organizations pay only for the resources they use. Efficient scaling ensures that resources

are not being paid for when they're not needed, leading directly to cost savings.

Elasticity and Responsiveness

- **Enhancing Application Elasticity**: Automated scaling enhances the elasticity of applications deployed in the cloud. Elasticity refers to the ability of an application to efficiently and quickly scale out (or in) in response to workload changes.
- **Improving Application Responsiveness**: As demand fluctuates, the ability of the system to rapidly allocate or deallocate resources ensures that applications remain responsive and performant. This is particularly important for customer-facing applications where user experience is critical.
- **Business Agility**: This approach also contributes to overall business agility. It enables organizations to respond quickly to market changes and customer demands without the constraints of fixed resource limits.

Conclusion

In hybrid cloud environments, automated scaling is an essential strategy for ensuring that applications are responsive, efficient, and cost-effective. By dynamically adjusting resources to match demand, organizations can maximize the performance and availability of their applications while optimizing costs. This capability is a key advantage of cloud computing, offering businesses the flexibility and agility needed to thrive in dynamic market conditions.

8.3. Balancing Workloads Between Mainframes and Cloud Infrastructure

Balancing workloads between mainframes and cloud infrastructure is a strategic task in hybrid cloud environments. It involves careful assessment and distribution of workloads to leverage the unique strengths of each platform. Effective management ensures optimal performance, cost-efficiency, and alignment with business objectives. Let's explore the key strategies for balancing workloads:

Workload Assessment and Distribution

- **Understanding Workload Characteristics**: Start by assessing the nature and requirements of each workload. Consider factors such as processing power needed, data sensitivity, scalability requirements, and how critical the workload is to business operations.
- **Strategic Distribution**: Allocate workloads based on the strengths of each platform. Mainframes are typically well-suited for high-volume transaction processing and workloads requiring robust security and reliability. Cloud systems, on the other hand, are ideal for scalable, flexible workloads and those requiring rapid development and

deployment.

- **Performance Considerations**: Consider the performance characteristics of workloads. Some may perform better on mainframes due to their architecture, while others might benefit from the cloud's distributed computing model.

Hybrid Cloud Management Platforms

- **Seamless Workload Mobility**: Utilize hybrid cloud management platforms that allow for the seamless movement of workloads between mainframe and cloud environments. These platforms can help manage complexities and ensure smooth operations across the hybrid landscape.
- **Automated Workload Placement**: Look for platforms that offer automated workload placement based on predefined criteria such as performance, cost, and availability. This automation can greatly enhance operational efficiency.
- **Integrated Management Tools**: Choose management platforms that provide a unified view of resources and workloads across both environments. Integrated tools simplify management and can offer insights for better decision-making.

Continuous Balancing and Optimization

- **Regular Review of Workloads**: Continuously monitor and review the distribution of workloads. As business needs and technology capabilities change, adjustments may be needed to maintain optimal balance and performance.
- **Adaptive Strategies**: Develop adaptive strategies that

allow for flexibility in workload placement. This includes being able to quickly respond to changes such as spikes in demand, new business opportunities, or evolving security requirements.

- **Performance and Cost Monitoring**: Keep an eye on both performance metrics and cost implications of workload placement. Regular optimization ensures that the organization is getting the maximum return on its investment in both mainframe and cloud technologies.

Conclusion

Balancing workloads between mainframes and cloud infrastructure in a hybrid environment requires a thoughtful and strategic approach. By assessing workloads, utilizing hybrid cloud management platforms, and continuously optimizing workload distribution, organizations can ensure they are leveraging the right mix of stability, scalability, and innovation. This balance is crucial for maintaining high performance, optimizing costs, and aligning IT infrastructure with business goals.

Workload Assessment and Distribution

Effectively assessing and distributing workloads in a hybrid cloud environment is key to leveraging the respective strengths of mainframes and cloud systems. This strategic allocation not only optimizes performance but also aligns IT capabilities with business needs. Let's break down the essential steps in this process:

Understanding Workload Characteristics

- **Analyzing Requirements**: Begin with a thorough analysis of each workload. Understand the computational demands, storage needs, and network requirements. This includes considering the amount of processing power and memory required for optimal performance.
- **Data Sensitivity and Security**: Assess the sensitivity of the data being processed. Workloads dealing with highly sensitive or regulated data might be better suited for mainframes, known for their security and data protection capabilities.
- **Scalability and Flexibility Needs**: Evaluate the scalability needs of each workload. Workloads with variable demands or those that need to scale rapidly are often more suited for cloud environments due to their elastic nature.

Strategic Distribution

- **Leveraging Mainframe Strengths**: Utilize mainframes for workloads that require high reliability, security, and capability to handle large volumes of transactions. This includes mission-critical applications that are central to business operations.
- **Exploiting Cloud Advantages**: Allocate workloads that require flexibility, scalability, and quick deployment to

cloud systems. The cloud is also ideal for workloads that demand modern, cloud-native features such as microservices or serverless computing.

- **Hybrid Workload Alignment**: Some workloads might benefit from a hybrid approach, where parts of the workload are handled by mainframes while others are offloaded to the cloud.

Performance Considerations

- **Optimizing for Performance**: Understand how different workloads perform on mainframes versus cloud systems. Some applications may inherently perform better on mainframes due to their architectural efficiencies, while others might take advantage of the cloud's distributed nature.
- **Load Balancing**: Balance workloads to prevent overburdening a single system. Proper load balancing ensures that both mainframes and cloud systems operate efficiently, without underutilization or overloading.
- **Monitoring and Adjusting**: Continuously monitor the performance and adjust workload distribution as necessary. Performance metrics can provide insights into how well workloads are running and whether they are in the optimal environment.

Conclusion

Assessing and strategically distributing workloads in a hybrid cloud environment is a dynamic and ongoing process. By understanding workload characteristics, aligning them with the appropriate platform, and continuously monitoring their performance, organizations can ensure that their IT infrastructure is not only efficient and cost-effective but also robust and responsive to the changing needs of the business. This strategic approach enables organizations to make the most of their hybrid IT investments.

Hybrid Cloud Management Platforms

Hybrid cloud management platforms play a pivotal role in effectively managing and orchestrating workloads across both mainframe and cloud environments. These platforms are designed to handle the intricacies of hybrid infrastructures, ensuring seamless operation and optimal resource utilization. Let's delve into the key features and benefits of using hybrid cloud management platforms:

Seamless Workload Mobility

- **Facilitating Cross-Environment Movement**: Hybrid cloud management platforms are engineered to enable the smooth transfer of workloads between mainframe and cloud environments. This capability is crucial for maintaining flexibility in how and where workloads are processed.
- **Minimizing Complexity**: By managing the underlying complexities, these platforms ensure that the movement of workloads does not disrupt operations. They handle the technical details, allowing IT teams to focus on strategic initiatives rather than on the nuances of workload migration.

Automated Workload Placement

- **Intelligent Resource Allocation**: Advanced platforms can automate the placement of workloads based on a set of predefined criteria, such as performance requirements, cost considerations, and availability targets. This intelligent allocation helps in utilizing resources in the most efficient manner.
- **Dynamic Adjustment**: The ability to dynamically adjust workload placement in response to changing conditions is

a significant advantage. For instance, a platform might automatically shift workloads to the cloud during peak demand periods and then back to the mainframe during off-peak times.

- **Enhancing Operational Efficiency**: Automation reduces the manual effort required to manage workload placement, thereby enhancing overall operational efficiency and reducing the potential for human error.

Integrated Management Tools

- **Unified Operations View**: Choose platforms that offer a comprehensive, integrated view of all resources and workloads, regardless of whether they are on the mainframe or in the cloud. This unified view is essential for effective management and monitoring.
- **Simplifying Management Tasks**: Integrated management tools simplify the complexity associated with running a hybrid environment. They provide a single pane of glass for managing diverse resources, streamlining administrative tasks.
- **Data-Driven Insights**: These platforms often come equipped with analytics and reporting tools that provide valuable insights into resource utilization, performance metrics, and operational costs. This data can inform better decision-making and strategic planning.

Conclusion

Hybrid cloud management platforms are essential tools for organizations operating in hybrid cloud environments, providing seamless workload mobility, automated workload placement, and integrated management capabilities. By leveraging these platforms, businesses can efficiently manage their hybrid infrastructure, ensuring optimal performance, cost-effectiveness, and alignment with their broader IT and business strategies. These platforms enable organizations to harness the full potential of their diverse IT ecosystems, fostering agility and innovation.

Continuous Balancing and Optimization

Continuous balancing and optimization of workloads in a hybrid cloud environment is essential for maintaining efficiency, performance, and cost-effectiveness. As business needs and technology landscapes evolve, it's important to adapt and optimize workload distribution regularly. Let's explore the key strategies to achieve continuous balancing and optimization:

Regular Review of Workloads

- **Ongoing Monitoring**: Implement a system for continuous monitoring of workload performance across both mainframes and cloud environments. This should include tracking resource utilization, throughput, and response times.
- **Responsive Adjustments**: Be prepared to make timely adjustments to the distribution of workloads based on the insights gained from ongoing monitoring. This ensures that workloads are always running in the most suitable environment.
- **Alignment with Business Objectives**: Regularly review whether the current workload distribution aligns with the organization's changing business objectives and strategies. This alignment is crucial for ensuring that the IT infrastructure supports business goals effectively.

Adaptive Strategies

- **Flexible Workload Management**: Develop strategies that allow for the flexibility and agility in shifting workloads. This flexibility is key to responding quickly to changes in demand, operational requirements, or market conditions.
- **Rapid Response to Demand Fluctuations**: Ensure that

your infrastructure can quickly adapt to spikes or drops in demand. For instance, utilize cloud scalability to handle sudden increases in workload, and rely on mainframe stability for consistent, high-volume processing.

- **Scenario Planning**: Regularly engage in scenario planning to anticipate how different situations, such as market shifts or new business initiatives, might affect workload distribution and infrastructure requirements.

Performance and Cost Monitoring

- **Balancing Performance and Expense**: Continuously monitor both the performance of workloads and the costs associated with their placement. Optimizing for one without considering the other could lead to suboptimal outcomes.
- **Cost-Effective Resource Utilization**: Analyze whether resources are being used in a cost-effective manner. This includes evaluating cloud usage costs against mainframe operational costs and looking for ways to optimize spending.
- **Regular Reporting and Analysis**: Establish a routine for regular reporting and analysis of performance and cost metrics. This data should inform decisions about workload distribution, resource allocation, and infrastructure investments.

Conclusion

Continuous balancing and optimization in a hybrid cloud environment require a dynamic and proactive approach. By regularly reviewing workloads, adopting flexible strategies, and closely monitoring performance and costs, organizations can ensure that their infrastructure is not only efficient and effective but also aligned with their evolving business needs. This ongoing process is key to maximizing the benefits of both mainframe and cloud technologies, ensuring they work in tandem to support the organization's objectives.

Chapter 9: Case Studies: Successful Mainframe and Hybrid Cloud Integrations

In this chapter, we'll explore a series of case studies highlighting successful integrations of mainframe systems with hybrid cloud environments across various industries. These real-world examples will provide insights into the strategies, challenges, and outcomes of such integrations. We'll also distill key lessons learned and best practices that can be applied broadly to similar initiatives.

Industry Examples of Mainframe and Hybrid Cloud Integration

- **Financial Services**: A case study from a major bank that integrated its mainframe systems with a cloud environment to handle increased digital banking traffic, enhance security, and improve customer service.
- **Healthcare Sector**: An example of a healthcare provider using hybrid cloud integration to manage patient data. The mainframe handles sensitive patient records with high security, while cloud components are used for analytics and patient engagement platforms.
- **Retail Industry**: A retail giant's journey in integrating their legacy mainframe systems with cloud services to

manage their supply chain more efficiently and enhance the customer shopping experience.

Lessons Learned and Best Practices from Real-World Implementations

- **Strategic Planning is Key**: Highlighting the importance of thorough planning before undertaking integration projects. This includes understanding business objectives, assessing IT infrastructure, and setting clear goals.
- **Flexibility and Scalability**: Insights into how hybrid cloud environments provided businesses with the flexibility to scale resources as per demand, especially during peak business periods.
- **Security and Compliance**: Lessons on maintaining robust security and compliance, especially when sensitive data is involved. Strategies employed by organizations to ensure data integrity and security during the transition and in the integrated environment.
- **Cultural and Organizational Changes**: Discussing the cultural shifts and organizational changes necessary for successful integration, such as adopting new work methodologies, continuous learning, and collaboration across IT and business teams.
- **Ongoing Management and Optimization**: Best practices in managing hybrid environments post-integration, including continuous monitoring, performance optimization, and regular reviews to align IT infrastructure with evolving business needs.

Conclusion

The case studies in this chapter provide valuable insights into the practical aspects of integrating mainframe systems with hybrid cloud environments. By examining real-world examples across different industries, readers can gain a deeper understanding of the challenges, strategies, and benefits associated with such integrations. The lessons learned and best practices outlined offer guidance for organizations looking to embark on their own integration journeys, ensuring they are well-equipped to leverage the full potential of their hybrid IT infrastructures.

9.1. Industry Examples of Mainframe and Hybrid Cloud Integration

Exploring industry examples of successful mainframe and hybrid cloud integrations provides valuable insights into how different sectors are leveraging these technologies to enhance their operations. Here are three case studies across varied industries:

Financial Services

- **The Challenge**: A major bank faced challenges managing the surge in digital banking traffic, needing enhanced security and improved customer service.
- **Integration Strategy**: The bank integrated its robust mainframe systems with a cloud environment. This integration aimed to leverage the mainframe's reliability for core banking processes and the cloud's agility for handling digital transactions and customer interfaces.
- **Outcomes**:
    - Improved handling of increased digital banking traffic.
    - Enhanced security protocols by combining mainframe security with cloud-based innovations.
    - Better customer service through cloud-driven

analytics and personalized service offerings.

Healthcare Sector

- **The Challenge**: A healthcare provider needed to manage large volumes of sensitive patient data securely while also leveraging modern analytics and patient engagement tools.
- **Integration Strategy**: The provider used a hybrid cloud approach where the mainframe was responsible for securely managing patient records, and cloud components were utilized for analytics and patient engagement platforms.
- **Outcomes**:
    - Secure and compliant handling of sensitive patient data on the mainframe.
    - Enhanced patient care through cloud-based analytics and engagement tools, enabling more personalized and efficient patient interactions.
    - Improved data sharing capabilities with other healthcare providers and systems, facilitating better coordinated care.

Retail Industry

- **The Challenge**: A leading retail giant needed to modernize its supply chain management and improve the overall shopping experience for customers.
- **Integration Strategy**: The retailer integrated its legacy mainframe systems with cloud services to enhance supply chain efficiency. The mainframe continued to handle high-volume transactions, while cloud solutions were implemented for inventory management, customer data analytics, and e-commerce platforms.

- **Outcomes**:
    - More efficient supply chain management through real-time cloud-based analytics.
    - Enhanced customer shopping experience with personalized recommendations and seamless online shopping interfaces.
    - Improved inventory management, reducing overhead costs and improving product availability.

Conclusion

These case studies across the financial, healthcare, and retail sectors demonstrate the versatility and effectiveness of hybrid cloud integrations. By leveraging the strengths of both mainframe and cloud systems, these industries have successfully enhanced their operational efficiency, security, customer engagement, and data management capabilities. Each case study provides a roadmap for similar organizations considering hybrid cloud integration, highlighting the importance of strategic planning, security considerations, and the need for a balanced approach to modernization.

Financial Services

The case study of a major bank in the financial services sector illustrates a successful integration of mainframe systems with cloud technology, highlighting how hybrid environments can address specific challenges in digital banking:

The Challenge

- **Surge in Digital Banking Traffic**: The bank experienced a significant increase in digital banking traffic, driven by a growing preference for online transactions among customers.
- **Need for Enhanced Security**: In the financial sector, security is paramount. The bank needed to strengthen its security measures to protect sensitive financial data and transactions.
- **Customer Service Improvement**: With the rise in digital interactions, the bank recognized the need to enhance its customer service capabilities, especially in handling queries, providing personalized services, and ensuring customer satisfaction.

Integration Strategy

- **Leveraging Mainframe Strengths**: The bank chose to continue using its mainframe systems for core banking processes. Mainframes are known for their robustness, reliability, and high-level security, making them ideal for handling sensitive financial transactions.
- **Adopting Cloud Agility**: For handling increased digital traffic and improving customer interfaces, the bank integrated cloud solutions. This provided the agility needed to manage dynamic workloads and user

interactions efficiently.

- **Hybrid Approach**: The integration strategy was to create a hybrid environment where the mainframe and cloud systems work in tandem, each playing to its strengths.

Outcomes

- **Handling Increased Digital Traffic**: The cloud integration allowed the bank to handle the surge in digital banking traffic effectively, ensuring smooth transaction processing and user experiences.
- **Enhanced Security**: By combining the inherent security of the mainframe with cloud-based security innovations, the bank strengthened its defense against cyber threats and data breaches.
- **Improved Customer Service**: Utilizing cloud-driven analytics and AI, the bank was able to offer personalized services to its customers. This included customized financial advice, real-time transaction alerts, and efficient handling of customer queries.
- **Scalability and Flexibility**: The cloud's scalability helped the bank adapt to fluctuating demands, while the flexibility of cloud services enabled the introduction of new digital banking features and services.

Conclusion

This case study demonstrates how a financial institution effectively managed the challenges of increased digital banking demand and the need for enhanced security and customer service. The strategic integration of mainframe and cloud technologies in a hybrid environment provided a balanced solution, leveraging the strengths of both systems to improve operations, security, and customer experience. This approach serves as a valuable model for other financial services organizations facing similar challenges.

Healthcare Sector

The healthcare sector often grapples with the dual challenge of managing sensitive patient data securely while simultaneously embracing modern technology for improved patient care. A case study of a healthcare provider illustrates how integrating mainframe systems with cloud technology can address these challenges effectively:

The Challenge

- **Managing Sensitive Patient Data**: The healthcare provider needed a secure and compliant way to manage large volumes of sensitive patient data, adhering to strict regulations like HIPAA.
- **Leveraging Modern Technology**: At the same time, there was a need to implement advanced analytics and patient engagement tools to improve care quality and patient experience.

Integration Strategy

- **Hybrid Cloud Approach**: The provider adopted a hybrid cloud model. In this setup, the mainframe continued to play a crucial role in securely managing patient records, thanks to its robust security and reliable performance.
- **Cloud Integration for Advanced Capabilities**: Cloud components were integrated to handle analytics and patient engagement platforms. This allowed the provider to leverage cloud computing's scalability and advanced processing capabilities for data analysis and interactive patient services.
- **Balancing Security and Innovation**: The strategy was to balance the security and reliability of mainframes for

sensitive data with the innovative and flexible capabilities of cloud technologies.

Outcomes

- **Secure Patient Data Management**: The mainframe ensured the secure and compliant handling of patient records, providing a trusted environment for sensitive health data.
- **Enhanced Patient Care**: Cloud-based analytics tools enabled more personalized patient care. This included predictive health analytics, personalized treatment plans, and improved monitoring of patient health trends.
- **Improved Patient Engagement**: Cloud platforms facilitated more interactive and engaging patient services, such as online appointment scheduling, telehealth consultations, and patient portals for easy access to health information.
- **Better Data Sharing**: The integration improved data sharing capabilities with other healthcare systems and providers. This was crucial for coordinated care, research collaborations, and comprehensive health management.
- **Scalability and Flexibility**: The cloud's scalability allowed the healthcare provider to efficiently handle fluctuating data volumes and rapidly deploy new patient services.

Conclusion

This case study demonstrates how a healthcare provider successfully navigated the complexities of managing sensitive data while incorporating modern technologies for improved patient care. The hybrid cloud approach, combining the security and reliability of mainframes with the agility and advanced capabilities of the cloud, offered a comprehensive solution. This strategic integration model can serve as a blueprint for other healthcare organizations looking to modernize their IT infrastructure while maintaining the highest standards of data security and patient care.

Retail Industry

In the retail sector, integrating mainframe systems with cloud services can significantly enhance operations, especially in supply chain management and customer experience. A case study of a leading retail giant demonstrates this strategic integration's effectiveness:

The Challenge

- **Modernizing Supply Chain Management**: The retailer faced the challenge of modernizing its supply chain to meet the demands of a rapidly changing retail landscape, characterized by a need for speed, efficiency, and adaptability.
- **Improving Customer Shopping Experience**: There was also a need to enhance the overall shopping experience for customers, both in physical stores and online, to stay competitive in the market.

Integration Strategy

- **Leveraging Mainframe Strengths**: The retailer kept its robust mainframe systems for handling high-volume transactions, a common requirement in the retail industry, especially during peak shopping seasons.
- **Incorporating Cloud Solutions**: To modernize its operations, the retailer integrated cloud services for several critical functions:
    - **Inventory Management**: Implemented cloud-based solutions for real-time inventory tracking and management, enabling more accurate and efficient handling of stock levels.
    - **Customer Data Analytics**: Utilized cloud platforms to

analyze customer data, gaining insights into shopping patterns, preferences, and behavior.

- **E-commerce Platforms**: Enhanced its online shopping platforms using cloud technologies, ensuring scalability and a seamless user experience.

Outcomes

- **Efficient Supply Chain Management**: The integration of cloud-based analytics dramatically improved supply chain efficiency, enabling real-time decision-making and quicker responses to market changes.
- **Personalized Shopping Experiences**: Leveraging customer data analytics, the retailer was able to offer personalized shopping experiences and recommendations, enhancing customer engagement and satisfaction.
- **Seamless Online Shopping Interfaces**: The cloud-powered e-commerce platforms provided customers with a smooth and reliable online shopping experience, capable of handling high traffic volumes and providing real-time inventory updates.
- **Reduced Overhead Costs**: Improved inventory management led to reduced overhead costs, minimized stockouts and overstock situations, thereby improving the bottom line.
- **Enhanced Product Availability**: Better inventory management also resulted in improved product availability, both online and in-store, meeting customer expectations more effectively.

Conclusion

This case study exemplifies how a retail giant successfully modernized its operations by integrating mainframe and cloud technologies. The strategic use of mainframes for transaction processing and cloud services for inventory management, analytics, and e-commerce led to enhanced efficiency, an improved customer experience, and better inventory control. This approach serves as a valuable model for other retailers looking to modernize their IT infrastructure and operations in a competitive market.

9.2. Lessons Learned and Best Practices from Real-World Implementations

The successful integration of mainframe systems with hybrid cloud environments in various industries offers valuable lessons and best practices. These insights can guide organizations planning similar integrations. Let's explore these lessons and best practices distilled from real-world implementations:

Strategic Planning is Key

- **Understanding Business Goals**: Prioritize understanding the overarching business objectives that the integration aims to support. This ensures that the integration aligns with and drives the organization's strategic goals.
- **Comprehensive IT Assessment**: Conduct a thorough assessment of the existing IT infrastructure to identify capabilities, limitations, and areas for improvement. This helps in determining the most effective integration approach.
- **Goal Setting**: Set clear, measurable goals for the integration project. This includes defining what success looks like and establishing benchmarks for performance, efficiency, and return on investment.

Flexibility and Scalability

- **Adapting to Demand**: Hybrid cloud environments excel in providing flexibility to adapt to changing demands. Implement systems that can scale resources up or down based on actual usage, particularly beneficial during peak business periods.
- **Balancing Workloads**: Learn to strategically distribute workloads across mainframe and cloud systems to leverage the strengths of each, ensuring optimal performance and resource utilization.

Security and Compliance

- **Data Protection**: Maintain a strong focus on security, especially when handling sensitive data. Implement robust security protocols and encryption methods to protect data during transmission and storage.
- **Regulatory Adherence**: Ensure compliance with relevant regulations and industry standards, particularly for industries like healthcare and finance. This involves regular compliance audits and adhering to best practices in data management.

Cultural and Organizational Changes

- **Embracing Change**: Successful integration often requires a cultural shift within the organization. Foster a culture that embraces change, innovation, and continuous improvement.
- **Cross-Departmental Collaboration**: Encourage collaboration between IT and business units. This ensures

that the IT infrastructure supports business needs and that technological changes are well-understood across the organization.

- **Continuous Learning**: Invest in training and development for staff to keep up with new technologies and methodologies. This empowers teams to effectively manage and optimize the hybrid environment.

Ongoing Management and Optimization

- **Continuous Monitoring**: Implement continuous monitoring of the IT infrastructure to identify areas for improvement and respond promptly to issues.
- **Performance Optimization**: Regularly review and optimize the performance of both mainframe and cloud components. This includes tuning systems for better efficiency and exploring new technologies that can enhance performance.
- **Alignment with Business Evolution**: Regularly revisit the integration strategy to ensure it remains aligned with evolving business needs and technological advancements.

Conclusion

The integration of mainframe and cloud systems is a complex but rewarding endeavor. The key to success lies in strategic planning, embracing scalability and flexibility, maintaining security and compliance, adapting to cultural and organizational changes, and committing to ongoing management and optimization. By following these best practices, organizations can effectively leverage their hybrid IT infrastructure to support their current and future business needs.

Strategic Planning is Key

Strategic planning is fundamental in the successful integration of mainframe systems with hybrid cloud environments. It lays the groundwork for a project that is aligned with business objectives and is technically feasible. Here's a closer look at the key components of strategic planning in this context:

Understanding Business Goals

- **Alignment with Business Strategy**: Start by ensuring a deep understanding of the organization's broader business goals. The integration should support and enhance these objectives, whether they involve expanding market reach, improving customer service, or increasing operational efficiency.
- **Informed Technology Decisions**: Technology decisions should be driven by how they can support and advance these business goals, rather than technology for its own sake.

Comprehensive IT Assessment

- **Evaluating Current Infrastructure**: Conduct a detailed assessment of the existing IT infrastructure, including both mainframe and any current cloud deployments. Understand the strengths and weaknesses of the current setup.
- **Identifying Integration Challenges**: Look for potential challenges in integration, such as compatibility issues, data migration complexities, or skill gaps within the IT team.
- **Capability Analysis**: Assess the capabilities of your current infrastructure against what is needed to achieve the desired integration outcomes. This may involve

considerations of scalability, reliability, security, and compliance requirements.

Goal Setting

- **Defining Clear Objectives**: Establish clear, specific, and measurable goals for the integration project. This might include objectives related to system performance, cost savings, operational efficiencies, or business agility.
- **Setting Benchmarks**: Define benchmarks and key performance indicators (KPIs) that will be used to measure the success of the integration. These could include metrics like system uptime, transaction speeds, cost reductions, or user satisfaction levels.
- **Realistic and Achievable Targets**: Ensure that the goals and benchmarks set are realistic, achievable, and aligned with both the technological capabilities and the strategic direction of the organization.

Conclusion

Strategic planning is a critical first step in the process of integrating mainframe and hybrid cloud systems. By thoroughly understanding business goals, conducting a comprehensive assessment of the current IT landscape, and setting clear and measurable objectives, organizations can lay a solid foundation for a successful integration. This approach ensures that the integration not only meets technical requirements but also delivers real business value, supporting the organization's overall strategic objectives.

Flexibility and Scalability

Flexibility and scalability are paramount in the effective management of hybrid cloud environments, especially when integrating them with mainframe systems. These characteristics allow organizations to adapt to changing demands and optimize resource utilization. Let's explore these aspects in more detail:

Adapting to Demand

- **Dynamic Resource Scaling**: In a hybrid cloud environment, one of the key advantages is the ability to dynamically scale computing resources according to fluctuating demands. This is particularly beneficial during peak business periods, such as holiday seasons for retailers or financial year-ends for banks.
- **Cloud-Enabled Scalability**: Utilize the cloud's scalable nature to handle sudden surges in demand. This could involve automatically provisioning additional compute resources or scaling out application instances to maintain performance levels.
- **Cost-Effective Resource Management**: By scaling resources based on actual usage, organizations avoid the costs associated with over-provisioning while ensuring that sufficient capacity is available when needed.

Balancing Workloads

- **Strategic Workload Distribution**: Effectively distribute workloads between mainframes and cloud systems based on the specific strengths of each environment. For example, mainframes might handle large-scale batch processing and transaction management, while cloud systems manage more variable, interactive workloads.

- **Leveraging Mainframe Strengths**: Utilize the mainframe for its high processing power, security, and reliability. Mainframes are particularly adept at handling large volumes of transactions and data, making them well-suited for critical business operations.
- **Utilizing Cloud Flexibility**: Deploy workloads to the cloud that require elasticity, such as web applications or data analytics platforms. The cloud is ideal for workloads that need to scale quickly or that are more experimental in nature, where resources need to be rapidly adjusted.

Conclusion

In hybrid cloud environments, balancing the flexibility and scalability of cloud systems with the robustness of mainframes offers a comprehensive approach to managing IT infrastructure. By dynamically adapting to demand and strategically distributing workloads, organizations can optimize performance, enhance efficiency, and maintain cost-effectiveness. This approach allows them to respond agilely to business needs and market changes, leveraging the best of both worlds in mainframe and cloud technology.

Security and Compliance

Security and compliance are critical considerations in hybrid cloud environments, especially when integrating with mainframe systems. These aspects are paramount in protecting sensitive data and adhering to regulatory standards. Let's delve into the best practices for ensuring security and compliance:

Data Protection

- **Robust Security Protocols**: Implement stringent security protocols across both the mainframe and cloud environments. This includes using advanced encryption for data at rest and in transit, ensuring that sensitive information is protected from unauthorized access or breaches.
- **Regular Security Updates and Patch Management**: Keep all systems, including both mainframe and cloud components, updated with the latest security patches. Regular updates are crucial to protect against new vulnerabilities and cyber threats.
- **Access Control and Authentication**: Implement strong access control measures, including multi-factor authentication and role-based access controls. Ensure that only authorized personnel have access to sensitive data and systems.

Regulatory Adherence

- **Compliance with Industry Regulations**: For industries like healthcare, finance, and government, it's essential to comply with specific regulatory standards such as HIPAA for healthcare, GDPR for data protection in the EU, and PCI DSS for payment card security.

- **Regular Compliance Audits**: Conduct regular audits to ensure ongoing compliance with these standards. Audits can help identify potential areas of non-compliance and provide an opportunity to rectify them before they become issues.
- **Best Practices in Data Management**: Adhere to industry best practices in data management. This includes implementing data governance policies, regular data backups, and ensuring data integrity.

Additional Considerations

- **Data Sovereignty and Localization Laws**: Be aware of data sovereignty laws that dictate where and how data should be stored and processed, especially in global operations. Ensure that data storage and processing comply with the laws of the respective countries.
- **Incident Response Plan**: Have a robust incident response plan in place. In the event of a data breach or security incident, having a clear, well-practiced response plan can minimize damage and ensure rapid recovery.

Conclusion

Maintaining security and compliance in a hybrid cloud environment is a multifaceted endeavor that requires diligent attention to data protection and adherence to regulatory standards. By implementing robust security measures, ensuring compliance with relevant regulations, and adopting best practices in data management, organizations can protect their sensitive data and avoid legal and financial repercussions. This proactive approach to security and compliance is essential for building trust and maintaining the integrity of the IT infrastructure in a hybrid cloud setting.

Cultural and Organizational Changes

The successful integration of hybrid cloud environments with mainframe systems often necessitates significant cultural and organizational changes within an organization. These changes are essential to support the new technological landscape and ensure that the organization can fully capitalize on the benefits of this integration. Here's a closer look at these crucial changes:

Embracing Change

- **Fostering a Culture of Adaptability**: Cultivate an organizational culture that is open to change and innovation. This involves encouraging a mindset that views change not as a disruption but as an opportunity for growth and improvement.
- **Promoting Continuous Improvement**: Encourage a culture of continuous improvement where feedback is valued, and there is an ongoing effort to refine processes and technologies.
- **Change Management Strategies**: Implement effective change management strategies to help employees adapt to new systems and workflows. This includes clear communication, addressing concerns, and involving employees in the transition process.

Cross-Departmental Collaboration

- **Bridging IT and Business**: Facilitate collaboration between IT and business departments. This ensures that the IT infrastructure and technological advancements align with and support the organization's business goals.
- **Shared Understanding of Goals**: Promote a shared understanding of how technology supports the business

objectives. This helps in ensuring that technological implementations are driven by business needs and not just technological capabilities.

- **Interdepartmental Teams**: Form interdepartmental teams or committees to oversee integration projects. This can foster better communication, shared responsibility, and alignment of objectives across different parts of the organization.

Continuous Learning

- **Training and Development**: Invest in ongoing training and development programs for staff, especially in IT and related departments. As technology evolves rapidly, keeping the workforce up-to-date is crucial for the effective management of hybrid environments.
- **Encouraging Skill Upgradation**: Encourage employees to upgrade their skills and knowledge in areas like cloud computing, data security, and modern IT management practices.
- **Knowledge Sharing Sessions**: Organize regular knowledge sharing sessions where teams can learn from each other's experiences, discuss new technologies, and explore best practices in hybrid environment management.

Conclusion

Cultural and organizational changes are as important as technological upgrades when integrating hybrid cloud environments with mainframe systems. By embracing change, fostering cross-departmental collaboration, and investing in continuous learning, organizations can ensure a smooth transition to a hybrid model. These changes not only facilitate the successful integration of new technologies but also help in building a resilient, agile, and forward-thinking organization.

Ongoing Management and Optimization

Ongoing management and optimization are crucial for maintaining the efficacy and efficiency of integrated hybrid cloud and mainframe environments. As businesses evolve and technology advances, continuous attention to these systems ensures they remain aligned with organizational goals and operate at their peak. Let's delve into the key aspects of ongoing management and optimization:

Continuous Monitoring

- **Proactive Infrastructure Oversight**: Establish a framework for continuous monitoring of the entire IT infrastructure. This involves tracking system performance, resource utilization, and potential security threats.
- **Identifying Improvement Opportunities**: Use monitoring data to identify areas for improvement. This could include detecting inefficient resource use, identifying potential bottlenecks, or uncovering security vulnerabilities.
- **Rapid Issue Resolution**: Implement systems that not only monitor but also provide alerts for immediate action. This enables IT teams to promptly address issues before they escalate, maintaining system integrity and performance.

Performance Optimization

- **Regular System Reviews**: Conduct regular reviews of both mainframe and cloud components to ensure they are operating at optimal levels. This might involve analyzing system logs, performance metrics, and user feedback.
- **Efficiency Tuning**: Regularly tune systems for better efficiency. This could include optimizing database performance, adjusting storage strategies, or fine-tuning

network configurations.
- **Adopting New Technologies**: Stay abreast of new technologies and approaches that can enhance system performance. This might involve integrating new software tools, adopting emerging cloud services, or leveraging advanced mainframe features.

Alignment with Business Evolution

- **Adapting to Changing Needs**: As business strategies and objectives evolve, regularly reassess and adjust the integration strategy to ensure it supports these changing needs. This alignment is crucial for the IT infrastructure to effectively contribute to business goals.
- **Flexibility in Strategy**: Maintain flexibility in the integration strategy to quickly adapt to new business opportunities or market changes. This might involve scaling cloud resources, modifying data workflows, or integrating new applications.
- **Long-Term Strategic Review**: Periodically conduct a comprehensive review of the IT strategy in the context of long-term business plans. This ensures that the infrastructure not only meets current requirements but is also poised to support future growth and transformation.

Conclusion

Ongoing management and optimization of hybrid cloud and mainframe environments are imperative for modern businesses. By implementing continuous monitoring, regularly optimizing performance, and ensuring alignment with business evolution, organizations can maximize the value of their IT infrastructure. This proactive and strategic approach enables businesses to stay competitive, agile, and ready for future challenges and opportunities.

Chapter 10: The Future of Mainframes in the Cloud Computing Landscape

The intersection of mainframe technology and cloud computing is an evolving landscape, presenting new opportunities and challenges. This chapter explores emerging trends, the evolving role of cloud services in mainframe environments, and predictions for the future of this dynamic ecosystem.

Emerging Trends in Mainframe Technology

- **Modernization and Innovation**: There's a growing trend towards modernizing mainframe technologies, integrating them with advanced software and tools to enhance their capabilities and interoperability with cloud environments.
- **Increased Focus on Security**: As cybersecurity threats evolve, mainframes are becoming even more critical due to their robust security features. Innovations in mainframe security are likely to continue, keeping them relevant in high-compliance and security-sensitive industries.
- **Hybrid Architectures**: The trend towards hybrid architectures is growing, combining the reliability and processing power of mainframes with the flexibility and

scalability of cloud services.

The Evolving Role of Cloud Services in Mainframe Environments

- **Enhanced Integration Capabilities**: Cloud services are increasingly offering better integration capabilities with mainframe systems, allowing for seamless operation across the hybrid environment.
- **Cloud as an Enabler of Mainframe Scalability**: Cloud environments are being used to complement mainframe capabilities, especially in handling variable workloads and providing additional resources for compute-intensive tasks.
- **Mainframe as a Service (MaaS)**: The concept of Mainframe as a Service is emerging, where mainframe resources are offered in a cloud-like service model, providing more flexibility and cost-efficiency.

Predictions for the Future of Mainframes and Hybrid Cloud

- **Continued Relevance of Mainframes**: Mainframes are likely to remain a vital component of IT infrastructure in many large organizations, particularly those in sectors like finance, government, and healthcare.
- **Increased Adoption of Hybrid Models**: The hybrid cloud and mainframe model will likely see increased adoption as businesses seek to balance the need for scalable, flexible cloud solutions with the robustness and security of mainframes.
- **Innovation in Mainframe Accessibility**: Advances in technology may make mainframes more accessible to a broader range of businesses, potentially altering the

perception of mainframes as being only for large enterprises.

- **Cloud and Mainframe Synergy**: The synergy between cloud and mainframe technologies will continue to grow, with more tools and services being developed to enhance their interoperability and collective strengths.

Conclusion

The future of mainframes in the cloud computing landscape looks promising, driven by ongoing modernization, enhanced security features, and the growing adoption of hybrid architectures. As cloud services evolve to integrate more seamlessly with mainframes, and as mainframes adapt to new demands, this relationship will continue to offer robust, efficient, and secure solutions for complex IT environments. The key will be in leveraging the strengths of both technologies to create an agile, secure, and resilient infrastructure that can meet the challenges of the modern digital world.

10.1. Emerging Trends in Mainframe Technology

The landscape of mainframe technology is continuously evolving, adapting to new challenges and opportunities in the digital era. Several emerging trends are shaping the future of mainframes, particularly in their integration with cloud computing environments. Let's explore these trends in more detail:

Modernization and Innovation

- **Enhancing Interoperability**: A significant trend is the modernization of mainframe technologies to enhance their compatibility and interoperability with cloud environments. This involves integrating mainframes with advanced software and tools, making them more adaptable to modern IT ecosystems.
- **Leveraging Open Systems**: Modern mainframes are increasingly incorporating open systems and software, which allows for easier integration with a variety of cloud-based applications and services.
- **API Enablement**: Enhancing mainframes with APIs (Application Programming Interfaces) is a key part of this trend, enabling mainframes to communicate more effectively with cloud platforms and services.

Increased Focus on Security

- **Robust Security Features**: As cybersecurity threats become more sophisticated, the inherent security strengths of mainframes are being emphasized and enhanced. Mainframes have traditionally excelled in security, making them crucial for industries where data protection is paramount.
- **Continual Security Innovations**: The mainframe community is continuously innovating in security to keep up with emerging threats. This includes advanced encryption techniques, improved access control mechanisms, and sophisticated monitoring tools.
- **Compliance Advantage**: For sectors that are heavily regulated and require high levels of data security, such as finance and healthcare, mainframes continue to be a reliable choice due to their compliance-friendly security features.

Hybrid Architectures

- **Balancing Strengths**: There's a growing shift towards hybrid architectures that combine the reliability and processing power of mainframes with the flexibility and scalability of cloud services. This approach offers a balanced solution that leverages the strengths of both technologies.
- **Enhanced Scalability and Flexibility**: By integrating mainframes with cloud services, organizations can handle dynamic workloads more efficiently. This setup allows for handling stable, high-volume transactions on the mainframe while using the cloud for scalable, elastic

workloads.

- **Cost-Effective Solutions**: Hybrid architectures can also offer more cost-effective solutions by allowing organizations to use each technology in the most efficient way, reducing unnecessary expenditure on resources.

Conclusion

Emerging trends in mainframe technology reflect a shift towards more integrated, secure, and flexible IT environments. The modernization and innovation in mainframe technology, coupled with an increased focus on security and the adoption of hybrid architectures, underscore the ongoing relevance and evolution of mainframes in today's cloud-centric world. These trends indicate a future where mainframes continue to play a crucial role in enterprise IT strategies, particularly for organizations that require robust security, reliability, and high transactional processing power.

Modernization and Innovation

The modernization and innovation of mainframe technology are pivotal in ensuring these systems remain relevant and efficient in today's rapidly evolving IT landscape. Here's a detailed exploration of these trends:

Enhancing Interoperability

- **Integration with Cloud Technologies**: Modernization efforts are largely focused on enhancing the interoperability of mainframes with cloud environments. This involves updating mainframe systems with newer software and tools that facilitate seamless communication and data exchange with cloud platforms.
- **Hybrid Environment Support**: By enhancing interoperability, mainframes become more versatile within hybrid IT environments, supporting a range of workloads and offering the stability and security of mainframe systems alongside the agility of cloud computing.

Leveraging Open Systems

- **Adopting Open Standards**: Modern mainframes are increasingly embracing open standards and systems. This shift marks a departure from the traditionally closed mainframe architectures, opening up new possibilities for integration and application development.
- **Easier Integration with Cloud Services**: Open systems enable mainframes to more easily integrate with cloud-based applications and services. This flexibility is crucial for organizations looking to leverage the best of both mainframe and cloud technologies.
- **Expanding the Developer Ecosystem**: By adopting open

standards, mainframes become more accessible to a broader range of developers, fostering innovation and widening the scope of mainframe applications.

API Enablement

- **Facilitating Communication through APIs**: APIs are becoming a key tool in modernizing mainframes. They act as intermediaries, allowing for efficient communication between mainframe systems and other IT infrastructure, including cloud services.
- **Enhancing Mainframe Accessibility**: APIs make it easier to access and utilize mainframe resources, simplifying the process of developing applications that can leverage mainframe processing power and data.
- **Enabling a Range of Applications**: Through API enablement, mainframes can support a wider range of applications, from legacy systems to modern cloud-based services, enhancing their utility and effectiveness in contemporary IT ecosystems.

Conclusion

The modernization and innovation of mainframe technologies are centered around enhancing interoperability, leveraging open systems, and enabling efficient communication through APIs. These advancements are crucial for ensuring that mainframes continue to be a valuable asset in the current and future IT landscape, particularly as organizations increasingly adopt hybrid models that combine the stability and power of mainframes with the flexibility and scalability of cloud technologies. These trends not only extend the life and relevance of mainframe systems but also open new avenues for innovation and application development.

Increased Focus on Security

The increased focus on security in mainframe technology is a response to the escalating sophistication of cybersecurity threats. Mainframes, known for their robust security features, are evolving to address these challenges, ensuring they remain a steadfast component in sectors where data security and compliance are paramount. Let's delve into the key aspects of this focus:

Robust Security Features

- **Inherent Security Strengths**: Mainframes have always been recognized for their strong security features. As cybersecurity threats evolve, these systems are being further fortified to protect against a wider array of digital threats.
- **Industry-Specific Security Requirements**: Given their capability to handle large volumes of sensitive data, mainframes are particularly crucial in industries like finance and healthcare, where data security is non-negotiable.

Continual Security Innovations

- **Adapting to Emerging Threats**: The mainframe community actively innovates in the field of security to keep pace with emerging and evolving cyber threats. This ongoing innovation ensures that mainframes remain one of the most secure computing platforms available.
- **Advanced Encryption Techniques**: New and advanced encryption methods are continually developed and implemented in mainframes to protect data both at rest and in transit, ensuring that sensitive information remains secure from unauthorized access.
- **Improved Access Control and Monitoring**:

Enhancements in access control mechanisms prevent unauthorized access to critical systems and data. Sophisticated monitoring tools are employed to detect and respond to security incidents in real-time, further strengthening the security posture.

Compliance Advantage

- **Meeting Regulatory Standards**: Mainframes offer a significant advantage in meeting strict regulatory compliance standards, which is a critical requirement in many industries. Their ability to secure sensitive data and maintain comprehensive audit trails makes them ideal for sectors with stringent regulatory requirements.
- **Data Privacy and Protection**: With increasing concerns and regulations around data privacy, such as GDPR and HIPAA, mainframes provide a secure platform that helps organizations comply with these legal requirements.
- **Reliability in High-Compliance Environments**: The reliability and security features of mainframes make them a preferred choice in environments where data integrity and compliance are not just important but legally mandated.

Conclusion

The increased focus on security in mainframe technology underscores their ongoing relevance in today's digital landscape, characterized by complex cybersecurity threats and stringent regulatory requirements. By continually enhancing their security capabilities and ensuring compliance-friendly features, mainframes solidify their position as a critical asset for industries where data protection and security are of the utmost importance. This focus on security, combined with their processing power and reliability, ensures that mainframes remain an indispensable part of the IT infrastructure in various sectors.

Hybrid Architectures

The trend towards hybrid architectures, which synergistically combine mainframes with cloud services, is reshaping the IT landscape. This approach leverages the distinct strengths of both technologies to create a more robust, flexible, and cost-effective IT infrastructure. Let's explore the key aspects of hybrid architectures:

Balancing Strengths

- **Leveraging Mainframe and Cloud Advantages**: Hybrid architectures capitalize on the mainframe's reliability and processing power for critical and high-volume transaction processing, while utilizing the cloud's flexibility and scalability for other dynamic workloads.
- **Optimized Workload Management**: This approach allows organizations to strategically allocate workloads based on their specific requirements and the best-suited environment, ensuring optimal performance and reliability.

Enhanced Scalability and Flexibility

- **Adapting to Fluctuating Demands**: The integration of cloud services with mainframes provides a scalable solution that can quickly adapt to changing business demands. This is particularly advantageous for handling unpredictable or fluctuating workloads.
- **Innovative Use of Cloud Capabilities**: Organizations can use the cloud for its advanced capabilities in areas like data analytics, artificial intelligence, and IoT, while relying on the mainframe for core business functions. This creates a flexible environment conducive to innovation and agility.

Cost-Effective Solutions

- **Efficient Resource Utilization**: Hybrid architectures enable more efficient use of resources. Mainframes can be used for what they do best, while the cloud can be used for needs that require elasticity, thus avoiding over or underutilization of resources.
- **Reducing Infrastructure Costs**: By balancing workloads between mainframes and the cloud, organizations can reduce the costs associated with maintaining and scaling their IT infrastructure. This approach allows for a more dynamic allocation of budget and resources.
- **Optimization of Operational Expenses**: The pay-as-you-go model of cloud services, combined with the robust processing of mainframes, offers a cost-effective solution for managing a wide range of business applications and services.

Conclusion

The shift towards hybrid architectures represents a strategic approach to IT infrastructure, blending the reliability and power of mainframes with the agility and innovation of cloud computing. This balanced solution offers enhanced scalability, flexibility, and cost-effectiveness, making it a compelling choice for organizations looking to optimize their IT operations while preparing for future technological advancements and market demands. Hybrid architectures are not just a trend but a practical response to the evolving needs of modern businesses.

10.2. The Evolving Role of Cloud Services in Mainframe Environments

The role of cloud services in mainframe environments is evolving significantly, enhancing the capabilities of mainframes and expanding their utility in modern IT infrastructures. This evolution marks a pivotal shift in how mainframes are perceived and utilized in conjunction with cloud technologies. Let's explore these evolving roles in more detail:

Enhanced Integration Capabilities

- **Seamless Hybrid Operations**: Cloud services are becoming more adept at integrating with mainframe systems. This enhanced integration capability allows for smoother operations across hybrid environments, bridging the gap between traditional mainframe processing and modern cloud-based applications.
- **Simplified Data and Application Integration**: Advanced integration tools and middleware are making it easier to connect mainframe data and applications with cloud services. This simplification supports more efficient data workflows and application management across disparate systems.

Cloud as an Enabler of Mainframe Scalability

- **Complementary Workload Management**: Cloud environments are increasingly used to augment the capabilities of mainframes. This is particularly evident in scenarios where workloads are variable and unpredictable. The cloud can dynamically scale to accommodate these fluctuations, thereby enhancing the overall scalability of the IT infrastructure.
- **Support for Compute-Intensive Tasks**: For tasks that require additional computational power or resources beyond what is available on the mainframe, cloud services can provide the necessary support. This includes leveraging cloud resources for specific, resource-intensive processes or temporary projects.

Mainframe as a Service (MaaS)

- **Mainframe Resources in a Cloud Model**: An emerging concept in this space is Mainframe as a Service (MaaS). This model proposes offering mainframe processing power and capabilities in a manner similar to cloud services, characterized by flexibility, scalability, and a pay-per-use pricing model.
- **Increasing Accessibility and Flexibility**: MaaS can make mainframe resources more accessible to a broader range of organizations, including those that may not have the capacity to invest in or manage a mainframe system internally.
- **Cost-Efficient Mainframe Utilization**: By adopting a service-based approach, organizations can use mainframe resources more cost-efficiently, paying only for the capacity

and processing power they need, when they need it.

Conclusion

The evolving role of cloud services in mainframe environments is marked by enhanced integration, scalability enablement, and the innovative concept of Mainframe as a Service. These developments are transforming how mainframes are integrated into modern IT strategies, making them more adaptable, accessible, and aligned with the dynamic needs of today's businesses. This evolution underscores the continued relevance of mainframes in a cloud-centric world and their potential to synergize effectively with cloud technologies for optimal IT infrastructure solutions.

Enhanced Integration Capabilities

The enhanced integration capabilities between cloud services and mainframe systems are a critical development in the IT landscape, facilitating seamless hybrid operations and simplifying data and application integration. This evolution is pivotal in bridging the gap between traditional mainframe environments and modern cloud platforms. Let's explore these enhancements in more detail:

Seamless Hybrid Operations

- **Improved Interoperability**: The growing adeptness of cloud services in integrating with mainframe systems marks a significant advancement in IT operations. This enhanced interoperability allows for seamless operations across hybrid environments, effectively merging the robust processing power of mainframes with the agility and scalability of cloud platforms.
- **Unified Management and Operation**: Enhanced integration capabilities lead to a more unified approach to managing and operating hybrid environments. Organizations can oversee their mainframe and cloud resources through a single pane of glass, which simplifies administration and improves operational efficiency.
- **Bridging Technological Gaps**: This evolution is instrumental in bridging the technological gaps between the distinct architectures of mainframes and cloud systems. It allows businesses to leverage the full spectrum of their IT assets without the limitations imposed by technological incompatibilities.

Simplified Data and Application Integration

- **Ease of Connectivity**: Advanced integration tools and

middleware are simplifying the process of connecting mainframe data and applications with cloud services. This ease of connectivity supports a more fluid and dynamic IT environment.

- **Efficient Data Workflows**: With simplified integration, data can flow more efficiently between mainframes and cloud platforms. This efficiency is crucial for businesses that rely on real-time data analytics, reporting, and decision-making processes that span across different IT environments.
- **Streamlined Application Management**: The ability to seamlessly integrate applications running on mainframes with cloud-based services enhances the overall functionality and value of these applications. It allows businesses to augment their legacy systems with modern features and capabilities offered by cloud services.
- **Enhanced Flexibility in Application Deployment**: Organizations gain the flexibility to deploy and manage applications in the most appropriate environment based on performance, security, and cost considerations. This could mean running certain parts of an application on a mainframe while utilizing cloud services for other components.

Conclusion

The enhanced integration capabilities between mainframes and cloud services mark a significant step forward in the evolution of hybrid IT infrastructures. By facilitating seamless hybrid operations and simplifying data and application integration, organizations can more effectively leverage the strengths of both mainframe and cloud technologies. This advancement not only improves operational efficiency and data management but also ensures that businesses can remain agile and responsive in a rapidly changing technological landscape.

Cloud as an Enabler of Mainframe Scalability

The integration of cloud computing with mainframe technology significantly enhances the scalability and flexibility of IT infrastructures, especially in managing diverse and fluctuating workloads. This synergy allows organizations to leverage the strengths of both mainframes and cloud services effectively. Let's delve into the details:

Complementary Workload Management

- **Balancing Variable Workloads**: In scenarios where workloads are unpredictable and vary in intensity, cloud environments offer the perfect complement to mainframes. The cloud's inherent elasticity enables it to dynamically scale resources up or down based on real-time demand, providing much-needed flexibility.
- **Enhancing Mainframe Scalability**: By integrating cloud services, mainframes, known for their robust processing power and reliability, can effectively handle stable, high-volume workloads, while the cloud can manage more variable and peak loads. This combination enhances the overall scalability of the IT infrastructure, ensuring that workload demands are met efficiently.
- **Optimized Resource Utilization**: This approach allows for more efficient utilization of resources. Stable workloads can be processed on the mainframe, utilizing its powerful capabilities, while the cloud can be leveraged for additional capacity during demand spikes, ensuring optimal performance across the board.

Support for Compute-Intensive Tasks

- **Augmenting Computational Power**: For compute-intensive tasks or projects that exceed the mainframe's capacity or are not ideally suited for it, cloud services can provide additional computational power. This is particularly useful for ad-hoc projects, data analytics, or development and testing environments.

- **Leveraging Cloud Flexibility**: Cloud environments are well-suited for handling tasks that require rapid scaling or large amounts of resources for a limited period. This flexibility is a significant advantage, especially for projects with variable resource requirements.
- **Cost-Effective Resource Extension**: Utilizing cloud services for additional computational needs can be more cost-effective than scaling mainframe resources. The pay-as-you-go model of the cloud allows organizations to only pay for the extra resources they use, as and when they need them.

Conclusion

The role of cloud services as an enabler of mainframe scalability represents a significant advancement in the way organizations manage their IT infrastructures. By combining the stability and processing power of mainframes with the scalability and flexibility of cloud services, businesses can create a more resilient, agile, and cost-effective IT environment. This synergy allows organizations to meet the demands of a wide range of workloads more efficiently, providing a competitive edge in today's rapidly evolving technological landscape.

Mainframe as a Service (MaaS)

Mainframe as a Service (MaaS) is a novel concept that aligns the traditional mainframe computing model with the more contemporary cloud service paradigm. This approach represents a significant shift in how mainframe capabilities can be accessed and utilized by organizations. Let's explore the key aspects of MaaS:

Mainframe Resources in a Cloud Model

- **Adapting to Cloud Service Models**: MaaS proposes the delivery of mainframe resources in a cloud-like service model. This approach mirrors the flexibility, scalability, and on-demand nature of cloud services, providing a modern twist to the traditional mainframe utilization model.
- **Service-Oriented Mainframe Access**: Under MaaS, mainframe processing power and capabilities are offered as a service. This means organizations can access these resources over the network, similar to how they would use cloud resources, without the need for physical mainframe infrastructure on-premises.

Increasing Accessibility and Flexibility

- **Broadening Mainframe Accessibility**: One of the significant advantages of MaaS is its potential to make mainframe resources accessible to a wider array of organizations. This is particularly beneficial for smaller businesses or those in sectors where owning and maintaining a mainframe is not feasible due to cost or complexity.
- **Flexible Mainframe Usage**: MaaS allows organizations to leverage mainframe capabilities for specific needs without

the long-term commitment or investment traditionally associated with mainframe computing. This flexibility can be particularly advantageous for short-term, intensive computing tasks or for businesses with fluctuating computing needs.

Cost-Efficient Mainframe Utilization

- **Pay-Per-Use Pricing Model**: Similar to cloud services, MaaS typically operates on a pay-per-use model. This means organizations only pay for the mainframe processing power and capacity they use, offering a more cost-effective approach compared to the significant upfront and ongoing costs of owning and operating a mainframe.
- **Reducing Total Cost of Ownership**: By adopting MaaS, organizations can significantly reduce the total cost of ownership associated with mainframe technology. This includes savings on hardware, maintenance, and the specialized personnel required to operate mainframe systems.

Conclusion

Mainframe as a Service (MaaS) is a groundbreaking development, reimagining how mainframe resources are deployed and utilized. It offers the power and reliability of mainframe computing combined with the flexibility, scalability, and cost-efficiency of cloud services. As this model continues to evolve, it is poised to expand the accessibility of mainframe capabilities to a broader range of businesses, fostering new opportunities for leveraging this powerful technology in various industries and applications.

10.3. Predictions for the Future of Mainframes and Hybrid Cloud

As we look towards the future, the landscape of mainframe computing and hybrid cloud integration is poised for significant evolution. These developments are likely to reshape how organizations leverage these technologies, driving innovation and efficiency. Let's explore some predictions for the future of mainframes and hybrid cloud:

Continued Relevance of Mainframes

- **Sustained Importance in Key Sectors**: Mainframes are expected to maintain their vital role in large organizations, especially in sectors like finance, government, and healthcare. Their ability to handle massive transaction volumes and sensitive data securely makes them indispensable in these industries.
- **Evolving with Technological Advancements**: As technology continues to advance, mainframes are likely to evolve accordingly, incorporating newer capabilities while retaining their core strengths in processing power and security.

Increased Adoption of Hybrid Models

- **Balancing Flexibility and Security**: The hybrid model, which combines the scalability and flexibility of cloud solutions with the robustness and security of mainframes, is anticipated to see increased adoption. This model offers a balanced approach to managing diverse IT needs.
- **Enhanced Integration Strategies**: As integration tools and methodologies improve, the implementation of hybrid cloud-mainframe environments will become more streamlined, encouraging more organizations to adopt this model.

Innovation in Mainframe Accessibility

- **Expanding to a Wider Market**: Technological innovations are likely to make mainframes more accessible and cost-effective for a broader range of businesses, not just large enterprises. This could lead to a shift in the perception of mainframes, highlighting their utility for a wider array of applications and industries.
- **Mainframe as a Service (MaaS)**: The concept of Mainframe as a Service could play a significant role in this, offering the power of mainframe computing in a more flexible and scalable service model.

Cloud and Mainframe Synergy

- **Growing Interoperability**: The synergy between cloud and mainframe technologies is expected to strengthen, with more tools and services being developed to enhance their interoperability. This will allow organizations to more effectively leverage the strengths of both technologies in a cohesive manner.

- **Collaborative Innovation**: Joint innovations from cloud and mainframe providers might emerge, offering solutions that seamlessly integrate the two platforms and unlock new capabilities and efficiencies.

Conclusion

Looking ahead, the future of mainframes and hybrid cloud appears dynamic and promising. Mainframes are expected to continue playing a crucial role in specific sectors, while the adoption of hybrid models is likely to grow, driven by advancements in integration and accessibility. The synergy between mainframes and cloud technologies will foster a more collaborative and innovative IT landscape, enabling organizations to leverage these powerful technologies to meet their evolving needs effectively. As these predictions unfold, businesses will have the opportunity to explore new ways of optimizing their IT infrastructures and driving digital transformation.

Continued Relevance of Mainframes

The future of mainframes is shaped by their continued relevance and adaptability in a rapidly advancing technological landscape. Let's explore these aspects:

Sustained Importance in Key Sectors

- **Crucial Role in Critical Industries**: Mainframes have long been the backbone of industries where large-scale data processing, reliability, and security are paramount. This includes sectors like finance, government, and healthcare. Their ability to handle massive transaction volumes and sensitive data securely continues to make them indispensable in these areas.
- **Handling High-Volume Transactions**: In finance, for instance, mainframes are essential for processing large numbers of transactions quickly and securely. Similarly, in healthcare, they manage vast amounts of sensitive patient data, while in government, they handle critical public services and data management tasks.
- **Reliability and Security**: The unmatched reliability and advanced security features of mainframes are key reasons for their sustained importance. They are uniquely capable of minimizing downtime and protecting sensitive data, which is crucial in these critical sectors.

Evolving with Technological Advancements

- **Adaptation and Integration**: Mainframes are not static technologies; they have continually evolved to meet changing technological and business needs. As the IT landscape advances, mainframes are expected to integrate more seamlessly with new technologies, including cloud computing and artificial intelligence.

- **Incorporating Newer Capabilities**: Future mainframes are likely to incorporate advancements in areas like machine learning, real-time analytics, and enhanced cybersecurity measures. This evolution will enable them to continue serving as powerful computing platforms, suitable for modern applications and workloads.
- **Maintaining Core Strengths**: While evolving, mainframes are expected to retain their core strengths in processing power and security. This combination of traditional strengths with new capabilities will ensure their ongoing relevance in the IT infrastructure of many organizations.

Conclusion

The continued relevance of mainframes in key sectors is underscored by their unparalleled capabilities in handling large-scale, sensitive operations and their evolving nature. As technology advances, mainframes are expected to adapt, integrating new functionalities while maintaining their core strengths. This enduring relevance and adaptability solidify their position as a critical component in the IT infrastructure of various industries, especially those where reliability and security are non-negotiable.

Increased Adoption of Hybrid Models

The increasing adoption of hybrid models, blending mainframe robustness with cloud flexibility, is a significant trend shaping the future of enterprise IT infrastructures. This approach caters to a wide range of IT needs by balancing the strengths of both technologies. Let's explore this trend further:

Balancing Flexibility and Security

- **Leveraging the Best of Both Worlds**: The hybrid model is gaining traction because it combines the best aspects of cloud computing and mainframes. Cloud services offer scalability and flexibility, which are essential for handling dynamic workloads and supporting innovation. Meanwhile, mainframes provide unparalleled security and robust processing power, crucial for critical operations and sensitive data handling.
- **Meeting Diverse IT Demands**: This approach is particularly appealing for organizations with diverse IT needs. For example, they can use cloud services for developing new applications and handling peak loads, while relying on mainframes for stable, high-volume transaction processing.
- **Customizable IT Solutions**: The hybrid model allows businesses to tailor their IT infrastructure according to specific requirements, workloads, and strategic objectives, resulting in a more efficient and effective IT environment.

Enhanced Integration Strategies

- **Improving Integration Tools and Methods**: As the technology for integrating mainframes with cloud environments improves, the barrier to adopting a hybrid approach is lowered. Enhanced integration tools and methodologies simplify the process of connecting disparate systems, making it easier for organizations to manage a cohesive IT infrastructure.

- **Streamlining Hybrid Environment Management**: Advancements in integration technologies are making it easier to manage hybrid environments seamlessly. This includes better tools for data synchronization, workload balancing, and security management across mainframe and cloud systems.
- **Encouraging Broader Adoption**: With these improvements, even organizations that may have previously been hesitant due to the perceived complexity of managing a hybrid environment are finding it more feasible and beneficial to adopt this model.

Conclusion

The trend towards increased adoption of hybrid models is a response to the evolving demands of modern businesses. By balancing the scalability and flexibility of the cloud with the security and robustness of mainframes, organizations can create an IT infrastructure that is not only highly efficient and secure but also adaptable to changing business needs. As integration strategies continue to evolve, this approach is likely to become more prevalent, offering a strategic solution for managing complex IT environments in various industries.

Innovation in Mainframe Accessibility

The innovation in mainframe accessibility is a key trend that is reshaping the way businesses perceive and utilize mainframe technology. This shift is making mainframes more approachable and feasible for a wider range of businesses, not just large enterprises. Let's delve into the aspects of this trend:

Expanding to a Wider Market

- **Broader Accessibility**: Advances in technology are making mainframes more accessible to a diverse market. This includes small and medium-sized businesses that previously might have found the cost and complexity of mainframes prohibitive.
- **Cost-Effectiveness**: Innovations are not only about enhancing technical capabilities but also about making mainframes more cost-effective. This involves reducing the total cost of ownership, including initial investments, operational costs, and maintenance expenses.
- **Changing Perceptions**: As mainframes become more accessible, their perception as being exclusive to large corporations or specific industries is likely to change. This opens up opportunities for a broader range of industries and applications to leverage mainframe technology, recognizing its value in areas beyond traditional large-scale transaction processing.

Mainframe as a Service (MaaS)

- **Service-Based Mainframe Utilization**: Mainframe as a Service (MaaS) is an emerging concept where mainframe capabilities are offered as a cloud-like service. This model enables organizations to utilize mainframe resources on an as-needed basis, similar to how they would use cloud services.

- **Flexibility and Scalability**: MaaS provides the flexibility to scale mainframe resources up or down based on demand, offering a level of agility that traditional mainframe deployments might not easily support. This is particularly appealing for businesses with fluctuating computing needs.
- **Reduced Barriers to Entry**: By adopting a MaaS model, organizations can bypass the significant upfront investment traditionally associated with mainframe computing. This lower barrier to entry makes mainframes a more viable option for a wider range of businesses, fostering greater diversity in mainframe usage.

Conclusion

The innovation in mainframe accessibility, particularly through the Mainframe as a Service model, signifies a pivotal shift in the mainframe computing landscape. It opens up new possibilities for businesses of all sizes to leverage the power and reliability of mainframes in a more flexible and cost-effective manner. As this trend continues, we can expect to see mainframes playing an increasingly vital role across a broader spectrum of industries and applications, far beyond their traditional domains.

Cloud and Mainframe Synergy

The synergy between cloud and mainframe technologies is a crucial development in the IT landscape, promising to bring about a more integrated and efficient approach to enterprise computing. This synergy is characterized by growing interoperability and collaborative innovation, each playing a pivotal role in shaping the future of IT infrastructures. Let's delve into these aspects:

Growing Interoperability

- **Enhanced Compatibility**: The interoperability between cloud and mainframe technologies is expected to grow, driven by the development of more advanced tools and services. This enhanced compatibility is crucial for creating seamless hybrid environments where mainframes and cloud systems can communicate and work together effectively.
- **Integrated Management Tools**: The focus is not just on the ability to run workloads across both environments but also on developing integrated management tools that simplify the oversight and administration of these diverse systems. This includes unified dashboards, monitoring tools, and security protocols that work across both cloud and mainframe environments.
- **Facilitating a Cohesive IT Strategy**: Improved interoperability allows organizations to more effectively leverage the strengths of both mainframes and cloud services, creating a cohesive IT strategy that maximizes efficiency, scalability, and security.

Collaborative Innovation

- **Joint Solutions from Providers**: The future might see

Chapter 11: Conclusion

As we conclude our exploration of the intersection between mainframes and hybrid cloud, it's clear that this convergence is more than just a technological trend; it represents a significant shift in the landscape of enterprise computing. Let's summarize the key points, reflect on the ongoing evolution, and consider the future outlook.

Summarizing the Intersection of Mainframes and Hybrid Cloud

- **Synergistic Relationship**: The integration of mainframe and cloud technologies has created a synergistic relationship that combines the reliability and security of mainframes with the agility and scalability of the cloud. This synergy addresses a broad spectrum of business needs, offering a balanced approach to IT infrastructure.
- **Enhanced Capabilities**: Through this convergence, organizations can enjoy enhanced capabilities, such as improved scalability, flexibility, and cost-efficiency. The hybrid model allows for a more dynamic IT environment that can adapt to changing business demands and technological advancements.
- **Diverse Applications**: The intersection has opened up new possibilities for diverse applications, ranging from traditional transaction processing to modern, cloud-native

applications. It has expanded the horizons of what can be achieved with mainframe resources, especially when coupled with cloud technologies.

The Ongoing Evolution of Mainframe and Cloud Integration

- **Continued Innovation**: The integration of mainframes with cloud environments is an ongoing process, with continuous innovations in interoperability, security, and management tools. These developments are making it easier and more efficient to manage hybrid environments.
- **Adapting to Market Needs**: As the market evolves, so does the integration of mainframe and cloud technologies. This adaptation is driven by the need to meet the changing demands of businesses, including the need for more robust data analytics, AI capabilities, and real-time processing.
- **Focus on Security and Compliance**: With increasing cybersecurity threats and stringent regulatory requirements, the focus on security and compliance within these integrated environments remains paramount.

Final Thoughts and Future Outlook

- **Mainframes as a Staple of Enterprise Computing**: Mainframes are likely to continue playing a critical role in enterprise computing, particularly in sectors where security and high-volume transaction processing are crucial.
- **Expanding Accessibility and Use Cases**: Innovations like Mainframe as a Service (MaaS) and enhanced integration tools are expected to make mainframe technology more accessible and applicable to a broader range of businesses and scenarios.

- **A Future of Collaboration**: The future of mainframes and cloud computing is not about one technology superseding the other but rather about finding collaborative ways to leverage the strengths of both. This collaboration is anticipated to drive further innovations and solutions that are more adaptable, efficient, and aligned with business objectives.

Conclusion

The intersection of mainframes and hybrid cloud is a dynamic and evolving field, offering vast opportunities for organizations to enhance their IT infrastructures. As we look to the future, the continued convergence and integration of these technologies will play a key role in shaping the next generation of enterprise computing, driving efficiency, innovation, and strategic business growth.

11.1. Summarizing the Intersection of Mainframes and Hybrid Cloud

The intersection of mainframes and hybrid cloud represents a significant evolution in the world of enterprise computing, creating a synergistic relationship that marries the best aspects of both technologies. This convergence addresses a wide array of business requirements and offers a comprehensive approach to managing IT infrastructures. Here's a summary:

Synergistic Relationship

- **Combining Strengths**: The integration of mainframe and cloud technologies has forged a powerful synergy. The reliability and security inherent in mainframes, when combined with the agility and scalability of cloud services, create a robust infrastructure capable of addressing diverse business needs.
- **Strategic IT Approach**: This synergy facilitates a strategic approach to IT infrastructure, where the unique benefits of both mainframes and cloud services are utilized to their full potential, ensuring operational efficiency and business continuity.

Enhanced Capabilities

- **Scalability and Flexibility**: The hybrid model significantly enhances an organization's ability to scale and flex its IT resources. It allows businesses to quickly adapt to market changes, manage workload fluctuations, and embrace technological advancements without overhauling their entire IT infrastructure.
- **Cost-Efficiency**: The model promotes cost-efficiency by optimizing resource utilization. Organizations can leverage cloud resources for variable demands while relying on the stable processing power of mainframes for core functions, thus avoiding unnecessary expenditures.

Diverse Applications

- **Broadening Application Scope**: The convergence of mainframe and cloud technologies has broadened the scope of possible applications. It extends from handling traditional high-volume transaction processing on mainframes to deploying innovative, cloud-native applications that harness the flexibility of cloud computing.
- **Enabling Modernization**: This intersection has been instrumental in modernizing legacy mainframe applications, making them more compatible with today's digital business requirements. It opens up possibilities for integrating advanced analytics, AI, and IoT into mainframe-based processes.

Conclusion

The intersection of mainframes and hybrid cloud is a transformative development in enterprise IT, offering a balanced, versatile, and efficient approach to managing complex computing environments. As this convergence continues to evolve, it paves the way for businesses to leverage a mix of traditional and modern IT capabilities, driving innovation and competitive advantage in an increasingly digital world.

Synergistic Relationship

The synergistic relationship formed by the integration of mainframe and cloud technologies represents a significant advancement in enterprise IT infrastructure. This combination harnesses the distinct strengths of both technologies to create a more dynamic and robust computing environment. Here's a closer look at this synergistic relationship:

Combining Strengths

- **Reliability and Security of Mainframes**: Mainframes have long been valued for their unparalleled reliability and top-tier security features. They are particularly adept at handling large volumes of transactions and sensitive data, making them indispensable in industries like finance, healthcare, and government.
- **Agility and Scalability of Cloud Services**: Cloud technologies bring agility and scalability to the table. They enable businesses to rapidly deploy applications, scale resources up or down as needed, and embrace innovative technologies like AI and big data analytics.
- **Robust Infrastructure for Diverse Needs**: The integration of these two technologies creates a robust infrastructure capable of meeting a wide range of business requirements. It allows organizations to leverage the processing power and security of mainframes while enjoying the flexibility and modern capabilities of the cloud.

Strategic IT Approach

- **Leveraging the Best of Both Worlds**: This synergy enables a strategic IT approach where the unique benefits of both mainframes and cloud services are utilized optimally. Organizations can tailor their IT strategies to use each technology where it excels the most, ensuring greater efficiency and effectiveness in their operations.

- **Operational Efficiency and Continuity**: The combination of mainframes and cloud services ensures high operational efficiency. Mainframes provide a stable and secure environment for critical operations, while the cloud offers quick adaptability and resource optimization. This balance is crucial for maintaining business continuity in a rapidly changing digital landscape.
- **Future-Ready Infrastructure**: By integrating mainframes with cloud environments, organizations create a future-ready infrastructure. This setup is well-equipped to adapt to emerging trends and technologies, ensuring that businesses remain competitive and resilient in the face of technological advancements.

Conclusion

The synergistic relationship between mainframe and cloud technologies marks a significant evolution in how businesses approach their IT infrastructure. By combining the reliability and security of mainframes with the flexibility and scalability of the cloud, organizations can create a powerful, efficient, and adaptable IT environment. This strategic integration paves the way for operational excellence and positions businesses to successfully navigate the complexities of the modern digital world.

Enhanced Capabilities

The enhanced capabilities brought about by the hybrid model of integrating mainframes with cloud computing are transformative for businesses. This model significantly boosts an organization's IT agility and cost efficiency. Let's delve into these enhanced capabilities:

Scalability and Flexibility

- **Dynamic Resource Management**: The hybrid model allows organizations to dynamically scale IT resources in response to changing business needs. Cloud services provide the elasticity to quickly ramp up or down, accommodating varying workload demands without the need for physical infrastructure changes.
- **Adaptability to Market Changes**: In today's fast-paced business environment, the ability to swiftly adapt to market changes is crucial. The hybrid model facilitates this agility, enabling businesses to deploy new applications or services rapidly and respond to market opportunities or challenges effectively.
- **Embracing Technological Advancements**: With the cloud component of the hybrid model, organizations can easily integrate and experiment with the latest technologies, such as artificial intelligence, big data analytics, and IoT. This capability ensures that businesses remain at the forefront of technological innovation.

Cost-Efficiency

- **Optimized Resource Utilization**: The hybrid model allows for more efficient resource utilization. By leveraging cloud services for fluctuating or less critical workloads and utilizing mainframes for stable, high-volume processing tasks, organizations can optimize their IT spend.

- **Reduced Infrastructure Costs**: The cloud's pay-as-you-go pricing model can lead to significant cost savings, especially for variable or short-term projects. It reduces the need for large upfront investments and ongoing expenses associated with maintaining underutilized infrastructure.
- **Balanced Investment**: The model promotes a balanced investment in IT resources. Organizations can judiciously allocate funds between maintaining robust mainframe systems for essential operations and investing in cloud technologies for growth and innovation.

Conclusion

The hybrid model's enhanced capabilities in terms of scalability, flexibility, and cost-efficiency represent a paradigm shift in enterprise IT strategy. By leveraging the complementary strengths of mainframes and cloud services, organizations can create a more agile, responsive, and cost-effective IT infrastructure. This approach not only addresses current operational needs but also positions businesses to effectively navigate future technological landscapes and market dynamics.

Diverse Applications

The convergence of mainframe and cloud technologies has indeed revolutionized the scope and capability of enterprise applications, significantly broadening their range and enhancing their functionality. This fusion has not only reinforced traditional mainframe applications but also opened doors to modern, innovative solutions. Let's delve into these diverse applications:

Broadening Application Scope

- **From Traditional to Cutting-Edge**: The integration of mainframes with cloud technologies expands the application scope dramatically. Mainframes continue to excel in their traditional role of handling high-volume, mission-critical transaction processing. Concurrently, the flexibility of cloud computing allows businesses to deploy and benefit from innovative, cloud-native applications.
- **Leveraging Cloud Capabilities**: Cloud environments enable the deployment of applications that are scalable, flexible, and capable of utilizing advanced cloud services. This includes everything from data-intensive analytics programs to customer-facing web applications, all benefiting from the cloud's vast resources and capabilities.

Enabling Modernization

- **Revitalizing Legacy Systems**: A significant impact of this convergence is the modernization of legacy mainframe applications. By integrating these applications with cloud technologies, businesses can enhance their functionality, making them more aligned with current digital business requirements.
- **Integration of Advanced Technologies**: This intersection

allows for the integration of advanced technologies into mainframe-based processes. For instance, businesses can enhance their mainframe applications with cloud-based artificial intelligence (AI), machine learning (ML), big data analytics, and Internet of Things (IoT) capabilities.

- **Improving Agility and Innovation**: The ability to modernize legacy systems with cloud technologies equips businesses with greater agility and paves the way for innovation. Mainframe applications can now be more readily adapted to changing market trends, customer needs, and emerging technologies.

Conclusion

The diverse applications made possible by the convergence of mainframe and cloud technologies mark a significant advancement in enterprise computing. This blend not only enhances the range and functionality of applications but also empowers organizations to modernize their legacy systems and innovate more rapidly. As a result, businesses can now enjoy the best of both worlds - the reliability and security of mainframes, combined with the agility and cutting-edge capabilities of the cloud. This transformation is a game-changer, enabling organizations to stay competitive and agile in the fast-paced digital landscape.

11.2. The Ongoing Evolution of Mainframe and Cloud Integration

The ongoing evolution of mainframe and cloud integration is a dynamic and continuous process, reflecting the ever-changing landscape of enterprise IT needs and market demands. This evolution is characterized by relentless innovation, adaptation to market needs, and an unwavering focus on security and compliance. Let's explore these aspects in detail:

Continued Innovation

- **Enhancing Interoperability**: Innovations in the field of interoperability are central to the integration of mainframes with cloud environments. Advancements in middleware, APIs, and networking are making it easier for these distinct systems to communicate and work together seamlessly.
- **Advancements in Security and Management Tools**: There is continuous development of more sophisticated security measures and management tools. These innovations are crucial for maintaining the integrity and efficiency of hybrid environments, ensuring they are secure, manageable, and scalable.
- **Simplifying Hybrid Environment Management**: The

ongoing advancements in technology are simplifying the management of hybrid mainframe-cloud environments. This includes better automation tools, improved monitoring systems, and more intuitive interfaces for administrators.

Adapting to Market Needs

- **Meeting Business Demands**: The integration strategy is continually adapting to meet the changing needs of businesses. This includes accommodating the growing demand for real-time data processing, robust data analytics, and the integration of AI and ML capabilities.
- **Agility and Responsiveness**: The ability to quickly adapt to market changes is a key driver of this evolution. Businesses require IT infrastructures that are not only robust and secure but also agile and responsive to rapidly changing market dynamics and technological advancements.
- **Customizable Solutions**: The integration is moving towards offering more customizable and flexible solutions that can cater to the unique needs of different businesses, allowing them to stay competitive and agile.

Focus on Security and Compliance

- **Prioritizing Security**: In an era of increasing cybersecurity threats, the focus on security in the integration of mainframe and cloud technologies is more important than ever. Continuous enhancements in encryption, access control, and threat detection are paramount.
- **Adhering to Regulatory Standards**: Compliance with

regulatory requirements remains a top priority, especially for industries like finance, healthcare, and government. The integration strategy continues to evolve to ensure adherence to these stringent standards.

- **Proactive Compliance Management**: There is a growing emphasis on proactive compliance management within these environments. This involves regular audits, real-time compliance monitoring, and adapting to new regulatory changes promptly.

Conclusion

The ongoing evolution in the integration of mainframe and cloud technologies is a testament to the dynamic nature of today's IT landscape. Driven by a need for continuous innovation, adaptability to market needs, and a strong focus on security and compliance, this evolution is ensuring that businesses can leverage the best of both mainframe and cloud technologies. This integration not only addresses current enterprise requirements but also sets the stage for future advancements, ensuring businesses are well-equipped to face upcoming challenges and opportunities in the digital world.

Continued Innovation

The continued innovation in the integration of mainframe and cloud technologies is a key driver in the evolution of enterprise IT infrastructures. This innovation is focused on enhancing interoperability, advancing security and management tools, and simplifying the overall management of hybrid environments. Let's delve deeper into these areas:

Enhancing Interoperability

- **Middleware and API Developments**: Significant advancements are being made in middleware and API technologies, which are crucial for linking mainframe and cloud systems. These improvements facilitate smoother data exchange and functionality integration between these historically disparate systems.
- **Networking Enhancements**: Innovations in networking technologies are also playing a vital role. They are improving the way mainframes and cloud environments connect and communicate, ensuring more reliable and faster data transfers, which is essential for real-time processing and analytics.
- **Streamlining Communication**: The goal is to create an ecosystem where mainframe and cloud systems can interact with each other as seamlessly as possible, minimizing the complexity traditionally associated with such integrations.

Advancements in Security and Management Tools

- **Sophisticated Security Measures**: As hybrid environments become more common, there's an increasing focus on developing sophisticated security measures. This includes advanced encryption techniques, robust access control systems, and comprehensive threat detection and response mechanisms.

- **Management Tool Evolution**: Management tools are evolving to provide more comprehensive oversight of hybrid environments. These tools are designed to handle the complexities of managing resources across both mainframes and cloud platforms, offering enhanced visibility and control.

Simplifying Hybrid Environment Management

- **Automation and Efficiency**: The integration of mainframes with cloud environments is being streamlined through automation. This includes the automation of routine tasks, resource allocation, and even certain aspects of security and compliance management.
- **Improved Monitoring Systems**: There's a push towards developing more advanced monitoring systems that provide real-time insights into the performance and health of both mainframe and cloud components. This helps in preemptively identifying and addressing issues.
- **User-Friendly Administration**: Efforts are being made to develop more intuitive interfaces for administrators, reducing the learning curve and operational complexity. This includes simplifying the control panels and dashboards used to manage hybrid environments.

Conclusion

The ongoing innovation in the integration of mainframe and cloud technologies is shaping a future where these systems not only coexist but work together in a more integrated, efficient, and secure manner. These advancements are crucial in ensuring that hybrid environments can meet the growing and changing demands of modern businesses, offering scalability, agility, and robust security. As these technologies continue to evolve, they will play a pivotal role in defining the next generation of enterprise IT infrastructure.

Adapting to Market Needs

The adaptation of the mainframe and cloud integration strategy to meet market needs is a critical aspect of its evolution. This responsiveness ensures that IT infrastructures are not only robust and secure but also agile and capable of supporting the dynamic requirements of modern businesses. Here's a closer look at how this adaptation is unfolding:

Meeting Business Demands

- **Real-Time Data Processing**: As businesses increasingly rely on real-time data for decision-making, the integration of mainframe and cloud technologies is evolving to facilitate faster data processing. This allows organizations to react quickly to market trends and customer needs.
- **Robust Data Analytics and AI Integration**: There's a growing demand for advanced data analytics capabilities and the integration of artificial intelligence (AI) and machine learning (ML). The combined strength of mainframe processing power and cloud-based AI and analytics tools can provide businesses with deep insights and predictive capabilities.
- **Supporting Evolving Business Models**: The integration strategy is aligning with evolving business models, including the need for digital transformation, e-commerce capabilities, and online services, ensuring that organizations can leverage their IT infrastructure to support these models effectively.

Agility and Responsiveness

- **Quick Adaptation to Market Changes**: In a fast-paced business environment, the agility to adapt to market changes is essential. The integration of mainframes with cloud environments is being tailored to offer the agility businesses need to respond to these changes swiftly.

- **Responsive IT Infrastructure**: The focus is on creating an IT infrastructure that is not just stable and secure but also quick to respond to new opportunities, challenges, and technological advancements. This is crucial for maintaining a competitive edge in the market.

Customizable Solutions

- **Tailored IT Solutions**: Recognizing that businesses have unique needs, the integration of mainframe and cloud technologies is moving towards more customizable solutions. This allows businesses to tailor their IT infrastructure to their specific requirements.
- **Flexibility for Different Industries**: Different industries have varying IT needs. The integration strategy is evolving to offer solutions that are flexible enough to cater to these diverse requirements, whether it's for a retail giant needing scalable e-commerce solutions or a financial institution requiring robust security for transaction processing.
- **Empowering Businesses**: By offering more customizable and flexible solutions, the integration empowers businesses to innovate and grow. This flexibility ensures that businesses of all sizes can leverage the power of mainframe and cloud technologies in a way that best suits their operational needs.

Conclusion

The ongoing adaptation of the mainframe and cloud integration strategy to meet market needs is a testament to its vitality and relevance in the modern business landscape. By continuously evolving to offer real-time data processing, advanced analytics, AI capabilities, agility, and customizable solutions, this integration ensures that businesses are equipped with an IT infrastructure that supports their growth, innovation, and competitiveness in an ever-changing market.

Focus on Security and Compliance

The focus on security and compliance in the integration of mainframe and cloud technologies is a critical aspect of their ongoing evolution. In a landscape marked by escalating cybersecurity threats and stringent regulatory requirements, prioritizing these areas is essential for maintaining the integrity and trustworthiness of IT infrastructures. Here's a detailed exploration:

Prioritizing Security

- **Enhancing Security Measures**: As cybersecurity threats become more sophisticated, the integration of mainframes and cloud technologies is intensifying its focus on security. This includes the continuous enhancement of encryption standards, access control mechanisms, and advanced threat detection and response systems.
- **Robust Protection Across Environments**: Given that mainframes often handle highly sensitive data, integrating them with cloud environments demands a security approach that is robust and comprehensive, ensuring that data remains protected irrespective of where it is processed or stored.
- **Balancing Security with Flexibility**: The challenge lies in balancing the inherently secure environment of mainframes with the flexible, scalable nature of cloud services, without compromising on the overall security posture.

Adhering to Regulatory Standards

- **Compliance in Sensitive Industries**: For sectors such as finance, healthcare, and government, where regulatory compliance is non-negotiable, the integration strategy is geared towards ensuring adherence to these regulations. This includes meeting standards like GDPR for data protection, HIPAA for healthcare information, and various other industry-specific regulations.

- **Evolving with Regulatory Changes**: As regulatory landscapes evolve, the integration strategies are also adapting to ensure continued compliance. This is crucial not only for maintaining legal and ethical standards but also for preserving customer trust and business reputation.

Proactive Compliance Management

- **Regular Audits and Monitoring**: There is an increasing emphasis on proactive compliance management in mainframe-cloud environments. This involves conducting regular audits, implementing real-time compliance monitoring systems, and establishing protocols for quick adaptation to new regulatory changes.
- **Ensuring Continuous Compliance**: The goal is to not only achieve compliance but to maintain it continuously. This requires a vigilant approach to monitoring regulatory landscapes, understanding the implications of new regulations, and swiftly implementing necessary changes in the IT infrastructure.
- **Integrating Compliance into Business Processes**: Compliance management is being integrated into the broader business processes, ensuring that it is not an afterthought but a fundamental aspect of the IT strategy.

Conclusion

In the current era, where data security and regulatory compliance are more critical than ever, the integration of mainframe and cloud technologies places a strong emphasis on these aspects. By prioritizing robust security measures, adhering to regulatory standards, and adopting a proactive approach to compliance management, this integration ensures that enterprises can leverage the combined strengths of mainframes and cloud technologies in a secure, compliant, and trustworthy manner. This focus is essential not only for protecting data and systems but also for building and maintaining the trust of customers and stakeholders in an increasingly digital world.

11.3. Final Thoughts and Future Outlook

As we consider the future of enterprise computing, the evolving role of mainframes in conjunction with cloud technologies paints a picture of continued relevance, increased accessibility, and collaborative innovation. Let's reflect on these final thoughts and the future outlook:

Mainframes as a Staple of Enterprise Computing

- **Continued Importance**: Mainframes are poised to remain a cornerstone in enterprise computing, especially in industries where their strengths – security, reliability, and the capacity for high-volume transaction processing – are indispensable. Industries like finance, healthcare, and government, which handle sensitive data and require robust processing capabilities, will likely continue to rely heavily on mainframe technology.
- **Evolving with Technological Advances**: As technology advances, so too will mainframes, evolving to meet contemporary challenges while maintaining their core strengths. This evolution will ensure their ongoing relevance in a rapidly changing digital landscape.

Expanding Accessibility and Use Cases

- **Mainframe as a Service (MaaS)**: The emergence of models like Mainframe as a Service (MaaS) is set to democratize access to mainframe capabilities, making them more accessible to a broader spectrum of businesses. This service-oriented approach will allow even small to mid-sized businesses to leverage mainframe power without the need for significant capital investment.
- **Broader Application**: Enhanced integration tools will facilitate the use of mainframe technology in a wider range of scenarios, expanding beyond traditional use cases. This could lead to more innovative uses of mainframes, especially in areas that benefit from their processing power and security features.

A Future of Collaboration

- **Synergistic Approach**: The future of mainframes and cloud computing is shaping up to be collaborative rather than competitive. By leveraging the strengths of both technologies, businesses can create a more robust, flexible, and efficient IT infrastructure.
- **Driving Innovations and Solutions**: This collaboration is expected to spur further innovations and solutions that are adaptable, efficient, and more closely aligned with evolving business objectives. The integration of cloud agility with mainframe robustness could give rise to new capabilities and services that were previously unattainable.
- **Enhancing Business Competitiveness**: The collaborative evolution of these technologies will not only address current enterprise requirements but also offer businesses the tools and capabilities they need to stay competitive and

more collaborative efforts between cloud service providers and mainframe technology companies. By working together, these entities can develop innovative solutions that more seamlessly integrate mainframe and cloud technologies.

- **Unlocking New Capabilities and Efficiencies**: These collaborative innovations have the potential to unlock new capabilities and efficiencies. This could involve leveraging cloud-based artificial intelligence and machine learning tools in conjunction with the processing power of mainframes, or creating more robust disaster recovery and business continuity solutions.
- **Expanding Mainframe Applications**: Collaboration can also lead to expanding the range of applications and use cases for mainframes. This includes deploying modern, cloud-native applications on mainframe platforms or utilizing mainframes for emerging technologies like blockchain.

Conclusion

The increasing synergy between cloud and mainframe technologies heralds a new era of enterprise computing, where the strengths of both are leveraged to create more powerful, efficient, and versatile IT environments. As interoperability grows and collaborative innovations emerge, organizations will be able to adopt more agile and cost-effective IT strategies, tailor-made for the evolving demands of the digital age. This synergy is not just about technological integration but also about fostering a more holistic approach to enterprise computing, where diverse platforms coexist and complement each other, driving business growth and transformation.

agile in a dynamic global market.

Conclusion

In conclusion, the trajectory for mainframes and cloud computing is one of mutual enhancement and collaboration. As mainframes continue to be a staple in enterprise computing, their integration with cloud technologies will open up new avenues for innovation, accessibility, and efficiency. This evolution will play a crucial role in shaping the future of business IT infrastructures, driving enterprises towards greater adaptability and success in the digital era.

Mainframes as a Staple of Enterprise Computing

Mainframes have long been the backbone of enterprise computing in various critical sectors, and their continued importance is assured by their unique strengths and adaptability. Let's explore the facets of their enduring role:

Continued Importance

- **Indispensable in Key Industries**: Mainframes remain crucial in sectors like finance, healthcare, and government. Their unparalleled security and reliability make them ideal for handling sensitive data and executing high-volume transaction processing which are common requirements in these sectors.
- **Handling Sensitive Data**: These industries deal with vast amounts of sensitive information, where data breaches can have severe consequences. The robust security features of mainframes provide the necessary protection against such threats.
- **High-Volume Transaction Processing**: Mainframes excel in environments where there are massive volumes of transactions, such as in banking and financial services. Their ability to process these transactions quickly and reliably is unmatched.

Evolving with Technological Advances

- **Adapting to New Challenges**: Mainframes are not static technologies; they are continually evolving. As new challenges arise in the digital landscape, mainframes are updated with new capabilities to meet these challenges effectively.
- **Integrating with Modern Technologies**: This evolution

includes better integration with modern technologies like cloud computing and AI. For instance, mainframes are being enhanced to work seamlessly with cloud services, offering hybrid solutions that combine the best of both worlds.

- **Preserving Core Strengths**: While adapting to new technologies and trends, mainframes maintain their core strengths – processing power, security, and reliability. This balance of innovation and stability is key to their ongoing relevance.

Conclusion

Mainframes, as a staple of enterprise computing, continue to be pivotal in sectors where their specific capabilities are most needed. Their evolution alongside technological advancements ensures that they remain relevant, efficient, and capable of meeting the demands of modern enterprises. This enduring significance is a testament to the mainframe's adaptability and the ongoing commitment to its evolution in response to the changing digital landscape.

Expanding Accessibility and Use Cases

The expanding accessibility and broadening application of mainframes represent a significant shift in how these powerful computing resources can be utilized in the modern business landscape. Let's delve into these developments:

Mainframe as a Service (MaaS)

- **Democratizing Mainframe Access**: Mainframe as a Service (MaaS) is a transformative model that makes mainframe capabilities more accessible, particularly to smaller businesses that traditionally could not afford or justify the investment in mainframe technology. By offering mainframe resources as a service, this model breaks down financial and technical barriers to entry.
- **Service-Oriented Approach**: MaaS operates on a cloud-like service model, where businesses can use mainframe resources on-demand. This approach significantly reduces the need for upfront capital investment and the complexities associated with mainframe operation and maintenance.
- **Enabling Broader Adoption**: With MaaS, even small to mid-sized businesses can leverage the robust processing power and security of mainframes for their specific needs. This could be particularly beneficial for startups and smaller firms in data-intensive sectors like fintech or health tech.

Broader Application

- **Expanding Beyond Traditional Roles**: Enhanced integration tools are facilitating the use of mainframe technology in a broader array of scenarios, extending their utility beyond traditional roles such as large-scale transaction processing and batch processing jobs.

- **Innovative Use Cases**: With improved integration capabilities, mainframes can be used in more innovative ways, such as in big data analytics, real-time fraud detection, and complex simulations. The integration with cloud-based platforms also opens up possibilities for using mainframes in newer areas like IoT data processing and AI model training.
- **Leveraging Unique Strengths**: The broader application of mainframes capitalizes on their inherent strengths – like superior transaction processing speeds, reliability, and high-level security – in newer, more diverse contexts. This expansion is key to keeping mainframes relevant and valuable in a rapidly evolving technological landscape.

Conclusion

The expansion of mainframe accessibility through models like MaaS and the broadening of their application through enhanced integration tools are pivotal in redefining the role of mainframes in today's business world. These developments are not just about preserving the relevance of mainframes but about actively expanding their role and utility in diverse business scenarios. By making mainframe technology more accessible and applicable to a wider range of businesses and scenarios, the potential of mainframes to drive innovation and efficiency in various sectors is significantly amplified.

A Future of Collaboration

The future trajectory of mainframe and cloud computing technologies is increasingly collaborative, promising a union that capitalizes on the distinct strengths of each to foster innovation, enhance efficiency, and improve competitiveness. Let's explore what this future of collaboration entails:

Synergistic Approach

- **Combining Complementary Strengths**: The integration of mainframes with cloud computing is evolving into a synergistic approach rather than a competition between old and new. This collaboration involves leveraging the reliability and security of mainframes with the scalability and innovation of cloud technologies.
- **Robust and Flexible IT Infrastructures**: By drawing on the strengths of both mainframes and cloud platforms, businesses can build IT infrastructures that are not only more robust and secure but also highly flexible and scalable. This balance is crucial for adapting to varying business demands.

Driving Innovations and Solutions

- **Catalyst for New Innovations**: The collaborative relationship between mainframes and cloud computing is expected to be a driving force for new innovations. This could include the development of new cloud services specifically designed to integrate with mainframe systems or new mainframe features that complement cloud-based applications.
- **Unprecedented Capabilities**: The melding of cloud agility with mainframe robustness could unlock capabilities and

services previously unattainable, potentially revolutionizing aspects like real-time analytics, data security, and large-scale processing in cloud environments.

Enhancing Business Competitiveness

- **Meeting Current and Future Needs**: This evolving collaboration is poised to not just meet current enterprise IT requirements but also anticipate future needs. It enables businesses to stay ahead of the curve in a rapidly changing technological landscape.
- **Tools for Agility and Competitiveness**: As businesses face increasing pressure to be agile and responsive in a globalized market, having an IT infrastructure that combines the best of mainframes and cloud computing will be a significant competitive advantage.
- **Adaptability in a Dynamic Market**: The ability to quickly adapt to market changes, scale operations, and innovate are key benefits of this collaboration, enabling businesses to respond more effectively to new opportunities and challenges.

Conclusion

The future of mainframes and cloud computing is set to be marked by a collaborative and integrative approach, bringing together the best aspects of both technologies. This union is anticipated to drive further innovations and solutions, enhancing the capabilities and competitiveness of businesses in various industries. As this collaborative evolution unfolds, it will open up new possibilities for enterprises to thrive in a dynamic and increasingly digital global market.

Epilogue

As we reach the conclusion of our exploration into the convergence of mainframes and hybrid cloud computing, it's clear that we stand at a pivotal juncture in the evolution of enterprise IT infrastructure. This journey has illuminated not just the current state of these technologies but also the vast potential they hold for the future.

Reflecting on the Journey

- **From Past to Present**: We've traversed the landscape from the early days of mainframes, witnessing their evolution from room-sized calculators to modern, sophisticated computing powerhouses. Simultaneously, we've seen the rise of cloud computing, from a novel concept to a ubiquitous element of the digital age.
- **Synergy and Innovation**: Our exploration highlighted the emerging synergy between mainframes and cloud technologies, a union that promises enhanced efficiency, security, and scalability for businesses. This synergy is not just about integrating two technologies; it's about creating a new paradigm in enterprise computing.

Envisioning the Future

- **A Collaborative IT Ecosystem**: Looking ahead, we foresee a collaborative IT ecosystem where mainframes and cloud computing coexist and complement each other. This ecosystem will be characterized by continuous innovation, enabling businesses to leverage the unique strengths of both technologies.
- **Driving Business Transformation**: The integration of mainframes and the cloud will play a crucial role in driving business transformation. Enterprises will harness this power to not only streamline operations but also to unlock new opportunities in data analytics, AI, and real-time decision-making.
- **Adapting to an Ever-Changing Landscape**: As technology continues to evolve, so will the relationship between mainframes and cloud computing. Businesses will need to remain agile, adapting their strategies to leverage these advancements and stay competitive.

A Closing Thought

The story of mainframes and cloud computing is one of endurance, evolution, and collaboration. As we close this chapter, it's evident that the journey is far from over. The future will undoubtedly bring new challenges and opportunities, but also the promise of continued innovation and growth. As enterprises navigate this landscape, the lessons learned from the past, coupled with the advancements of the present, will be invaluable guides in forging a path to a successful, technologically empowered future.

Don't miss out!

Visit the website below and you can sign up to receive emails whenever Isaac Nangan publishes a new book. There's no charge and no obligation.

https://books2read.com/r/B-A-SPRBB-NGGWC

BOOKS 2 READ

Connecting independent readers to independent writers.

Did you love *Mainframes in the Hybrid Cloud Era*? Then you should read *Next-Gen Mainframe: Mastering Modern Automation Techniques*[1] by Isaac Nangan!

[2]

In the ever-evolving landscape of technology, the longevity and resilience of mainframe computers stand as a testament to their unparalleled reliability and efficiency. However, as the digital era marches forward, these robust machines face new challenges and opportunities. "Next-Gen Mainframe: Mastering Modern Automation Techniques" is a journey into the heart of modernizing these computing giants through the lens of automation.

This book is born from a dual realization: the undiminished relevance of mainframes in critical sectors and the transformative power of modern automation technologies. It's crafted for IT

1. https://books2read.com/u/m0aMkJ

2. https://books2read.com/u/m0aMkJ

professionals, mainframe administrators, and technology enthusiasts looking to bridge the gap between traditional mainframe operations and cutting-edge automation strategies.

As you delve into these pages, you'll embark on a comprehensive exploration. From the historic evolution of mainframes to the intricate workings of their architecture, we lay a foundation upon which the principles of automation are built. We dissect modern tools and technologies, providing insights into how artificial intelligence, machine learning, and cloud computing are revolutionizing mainframe operations. The chapters are peppered with real-world case studies, offering a glimpse into successful automation strategies and the lessons learned from them.

This book doesn't just aim to inform; it strives to equip you with practical knowledge and an understanding of emerging trends to prepare you for the future of mainframe computing. Whether you're seeking to enhance your professional skills or satisfy a curiosity about the intersection of mainframes and modern automation, this book offers a comprehensive guide to understanding and implementing these technologies.

As we stand at the cusp of a new era in computing, "Next-Gen Mainframe: Mastering Modern Automation Techniques" invites you to be part of the exciting journey of transforming mainframes into dynamic, automated powerhouses of the digital age.

Also by Isaac Nangan

Mainframes

Mastering z/OS Management Facility: A Comprehensive Guide to Mainframe Innovation

How to Harness the Power of Jenkins on Mainframes: A Comprehensive Guide

Mainframe Revolution: Harnessing AI for Next-Gen Computing

Encapsulating Legacy: A Guide to Service-Oriented Architecture in Mainframe Systems

Mainframe Revival: Embracing Containerization

Modern Mainframe Mastery: Navigating the New Era of Systems Management

Next-Gen Mainframe: Mastering Modern Automation Techniques

Mainframes in the Hybrid Cloud Era

www.ingramcontent.com/pod-product-compliance
Lightning Source LLC
LaVergne TN
LVHW052242200926
848481LV00002B/245
* 9 7 8 9 8 1 5 1 9 4 4 6 3 *